COME AWAY WITH ESG

Praise for the series:

It was only a matter of time before a clever publisher realized that there is an audience for whom *Exile on Main Street* or *Electric Ladyland* are as significant and worthy of study as *The Catcher in the Rye* or *Middlemarch* … The series … is freewheeling and eclectic, ranging from minute rock-geek analysis to idiosyncratic personal celebration
—*The New York Times Book Review*

Ideal for the rock geek who thinks liner notes just aren't enough
—*Rolling Stone*

One of the coolest publishing imprints on the planet
—*Bookslut*

These are for the insane collectors out there who appreciate fantastic design, well-executed thinking, and things that make your house look cool. Each volume in this series takes a seminal album and breaks it down in startling minutiae. We love these. We are huge nerds
—*Vice*

A brilliant series … each one a work of real love
—*NME* (UK)

Passionate, obsessive, and smart
—*Nylon*

Religious tracts for the rock 'n' roll faithful
—*Boldt*

A consistently excellent series
—*Uncut* (UK)

We … aren't naive enough to think that we're your only source
for reading about music (but if we had our way … watch out).
For those of you who really like to know everything there is to
know about an album, you'd do well to check out Bloomsbury's
"33 1/3" series of books
—*Pitchfork*

For almost twenty years, the 33 1/3 series of music books
has focused on individual albums by acts well-known
(Bob Dylan, Nirvana, Abba, Radiohead),cultish (Neutral Milk
Hotel, Throbbing Gristle, Wire) and many levels in-between.
The range of music and their creators defines "eclectic," while the
writing veers from freewheeling to acutely insightful. In essence,
the books are for the music fan who (as Rolling Stone noted)
"thinks liner notes just aren't enough"
—*The Irish Times*

**For reviews of individual titles in the series, please visit our blog
at 333sound.com and our website at https://www.bloomsbury.
com/uk/academic/music-sound-studies/**

Follow us on Twitter: @333books

Like us on Facebook: https://www.facebook.com/33.3books

For a complete list of books in this series, see the back of this book.

Forthcoming in the series:

Come Away with ESG

Cheri Percy

BLOOMSBURY ACADEMIC
NEW YORK • LONDON • OXFORD • NEW DELHI • SYDNEY

BLOOMSBURY ACADEMIC
Bloomsbury Publishing Inc
1385 Broadway, New York, NY 10018, USA
50 Bedford Square, London, WC1B 3DP, UK
29 Earlsfort Terrace, Dublin 2, Ireland

BLOOMSBURY, BLOOMSBURY ACADEMIC and the Diana logo are trademarks of
Bloomsbury Publishing Plc

First published in the United States of America 2023

Bloomsbury Publishing Inc does not have any control over, or responsibility for, any
third-party websites referred to or in this book. All internet addresses given in this
book were correct at the time of going to press. The author
and publisher regret any inconvenience caused if addresses
have changed or sites have ceased to exist but can accept
no responsibility for any such changes.

Whilst every effort has been made to locate copyright holders, the publishers
would be grateful to hear from any person(s) not here acknowledged.

Library of Congress Cataloging-in-Publication Data
Names: Percy, Cheri, author.
Title: Come away with ESG / Cheri Percy.
Description: New York : Bloomsbury Academic, 2023. |
Series: 33 1/3 | Includes bibliographical references. |
Summary: "Repositions ESG in their rightful place as punk pioneers and
explains how they have paved the way for modern dance music
today"– Provided by publisher.
Identifiers: LCCN 2022043212 (print) | LCCN 2022043213 (ebook) |
ISBN 9781501379192 (paperback) | ISBN 9781501379222 (epub) |
ISBN 9781501379215 (pdf) | ISBN 9781501379208 (ebook other)
Subjects: LCSH: ESG (Musical group). Come away with ESG. |
Post-punk music–History and criticism. | Funk (Music)–History and criticism.
Classification: LCC ML421.E78 P47 2023 (print) | LCC ML421.E78 (ebook) |
DDC 782.42166092/2–dc23/eng/20220916
LC record available at https://lccn.loc.gov/2022043212
LC ebook record available at https://lccn.loc.gov/2022043213

ISBN: PB: 978-1-5013-7919-2
ePDF: 978-1-5013-7921-5
eBook: 978-1-5013-7922-2

Series: 33 1/3

Typeset by Newgen KnowledgeWorks Pvt. Ltd., Chennai, India
Printed and bound in Great Britain

To find out more about our authors and books visit https://www.bloomsbury.com
and sign up for our newsletters.

For my sister, Carly, who also loved the beat.

Contents

Introduction

It was Spring 2020 when I spotted the open call for 33 ⅓ proposals. We were two months into a government-led lockdown during the early stages of a global pandemic. As the general public was ordered to stay home, gigs were swiftly cancelled, new release time lines pushed back, and live venues closed their doors across the UK. As a freelance writer with a strong steer toward women in music, this posed something of a problem. Many of my go-to magazine editors were no longer commissioning freelancers, or worse, furloughed entirely from their positions. My inbox was light on paying gigs. The call out for new book proposals then provided the perfect escape from the harsh realities of an arts culture in peril.

Selecting my chosen album was tough though. Should I set my stall out early with a riot grrrl classic or play more leftfield in honor of my (often indulgent) pop sensibilities? (Hindsight is a beautiful thing as, a few years later, my teenage heartthrobs Hanson would face extreme criticism from fans after an in-depth *VICE* investigation into their perceived conservative politics and uneasy silence surrounding 2021's Black Lives Matter protests.) But while the Tulsa trio might've skirted around their response to such deep-rooted marginalization, my intentions for this book were the polar opposite. As a British-born white woman raised by a Northern matriarch, I've always made the intention of my work to amplify the voices of underrepresented artists in the music industry. And when you put the brief like that, there was one band in particular that was long overdue a blast on the bullhorn.

I first spoke to Renee Scroggins, bandleader and elder sister of the South Bronx group ESG, in 2015 for a (sadly now defunct) music magazine dedicated to women and nonbinary musicians. She dialed into our call from her home in Atlanta on a cloudy Spring afternoon, grousing on the Georgia capital's variable weather. The band was heading back to British shores for what was being pegged as their final UK tour but Scroggins was awaiting knee surgery after a nasty fall from the tour van a year prior. When your band has been part of the live circuit for nearly forty years though you understandably become fairly resilient. (Case in point: at the Leeds show in question, Scroggins simply soaked the swollen limb, popped a couple of painkillers, and made it on stage the same night.)

This notion of resilience is a defining factor in the sister group that formed in late 1970s New York, propelled by their mother's belief that music could steer them away from the gang culture permeating the Bronx Projects where they lived. Since the group's benevolent formation, the story of ESG is littered with industry icons heralding the group as visionaries of their era, from Tony Wilson of Factory Records fame to late great club DJ Larry Levan. But even with all this touting from music industry titans, more often than not, your average music fan won't know ESG by name. But if you don't know the Scroggins sisters by name, you'll know their nature by some of the cornerstones of their career.

Early release "UFO" appeared as a bedrock to hundreds of hip hop songs. They were the first stateside band ever to release on the iconic Manchester indie label Factory Records—an institution we now all have wild ideas about having seen Steve Coogan's notable performance as the label's founder Tony Wilson in *24 Hour Party People*. The sibling troupe, much to Joy Division/New Order's Peter Hook's amazement, even opened up the night of The Haçienda's launch party in the Northern city. They shared studio time with the now infamous Martin Hannett on Wilson's watch too. You might recognize Hannett's name for the integral role he played in shaping the sound of cult band Joy Division. What's less documented is his time in laying down the sound that would permeate hundreds of songs and span into the next millennium of music making. In fact, the only reason that ESG's "UFO" landed on their first EP (extended play record) was down to Hannett leaving the tape running. Thanks to bonus reel time and Renee Scroggins's persistence that there was something in the unusual instrumental number, "UFO" soared from that first Factory Floor release and into the atmosphere.

ESG's influence can be felt across multiple time zones; it's there in the early 1980s performing alongside label peers Bush Tetras and on the fringes of the hardcore scene as New York newcomers The Beastie Boys sing the praises of the coolest band in town. Their strained guitar feedback provided the hook for countless chart-topping rap hits in the 1990s—tucked deep in the mix of Biggie Smalls' "Party and Bullshit" and in the crescendo for Public Enemy's "Night of the Living Baseheads." The noughties also notoriously reveled in the sisters' discography for inspiration, with LCD Soundsystem frontman James Murphy hunting out their LPs (long play records) among Liquid Liquid and Can in the vinyl crates. And New York siren and frontwoman of Yeah Yeah Yeahs Karen O attributes ESG as a defining factor on her own band's stripped-back dynamics.

For any other band, those admirable accolades would earn them a spot in Glastonbury's legends slot. At the very least, their name should appear documented in the reams of coverage of the early New York club scene in the 1970s when they began their careers. But much like the subject of their extraterrestrial single, ESG often remains unidentifiable in modern-day music. To hold such a position after nearly four decades of writing, recording, and producing music, unsurprisingly, has made Renee Scroggins more than a little irked by the industry.

These frustrations are deep-rooted, after being brutally introduced to the pitfalls of the music industry while still in her teens. Technically still underage at the time of "signing," she and her siblings joined the influential roster of cult indie 99 Records. But when it came to the label's deal with the band, founder Ed Bahlman's approach appeared to be more of a formality than any legally binding document—an arrangement that worked when the label was putting out ESG's early EPs and securing paid gigs across the city but not so much when the production eventually folds and you don't have the rights to your original recordings. 99 Records allegedly operated on this basis with their whole roster—managing, booking, and securing licensing with no written permission. According to Scroggins, one day Bahlman called his various acts into a meeting where he inexplicably dissolved 99 Records, advising them to also get out of the business, since his own disillusion had prompted him to quit.[1]

The exploitation only continued into their twenties with the band's trademark sounds being regularly used for samples over the following decade. First, there were the hundreds of hip hop artists who built chart-topping singles from the building blocks of that eerie guitar screech from early single "UFO," with little or no credit to its origin story. It's that lead lick that forms the hook for Big Daddy Kane's "Ain't No Half-Steppin," just one of the many contemporary artists who has lifted loops without paying the band. Not to mention that a lot of those nineties OGs weren't exactly preaching about parity over their scaling rhetoric, another factor Renee Scroggins has repeatedly refuted calling the reuse alongside such misogynistic lyricism "disturbing."

On the same early EP, fellow underground favorite "Moody" also became synonymous with the house music scene that launched in the early 1990s, thanks to Chip E. using the song's bassline for his 1985 single "Like This." The Godfather of House music is another hugely successful recording artist who failed to credit the band for that era-defying sound. But it wasn't just far-reaching figures in the music industry snatching these samples, as author of *God Save the Queens: The Essential History of Women in Hip Hop* Kathy Iandoli remarked; the exploitation was happening far closer to home. "ESG were [still] active in the scene. As fast as they were making something, someone was taking it."[2] It wasn't uncommon in the early 1980s for complete songs to become bootlegged and sold by 12-inch retailers without a penny of those sales going back to the artists who wrote and played the originals. So as the Chinese whispers of the credits trail ran into obscurity, the Scroggins sisters' names eventually faded into white label anonymity along with their dues.

You'd think that after all these fractious relationships with the industry ESG would be keen to step away from the limelight, but the group has been performing live, in various family-themed guises, for the last forty years, playing some of their first support slots alongside punk flag bearers like The Clash and venerable DJ Grandmaster Flash. The same backdrop might also lead you to assume that frontwoman and founder Renee Scoggins would appear more than a little disagreeable when it came to speaking with the media. Setting up my initial interview with her though, and subsequent conversations together for She Shreds back in 2018 (a former magazine and now online media platform dedicated to women and nonbinary guitarists), the bandleader came across as a charming storyteller, recounting her memories from the Christmas when she and her sisters received their first instruments under the tree to that opening night spluttering on sawdust between the scaffolding of Wilson's Manchester monolith.

So when I emailed Renee at the tail end of 2020 after hearing that my proposal had been accepted, I was quite surprised to find that the songwriter immediately appeared more defensive, specifically expressing her frustrations around incorrect information being written about the band. I began contacting some of ESG's 99 Records' peers to hear more about the early days of the New York scene, hoping to piece together as much of the story as possible before launching into my questions for the group. Vivien Goldman was an obvious choice, as not only a 99 alumna but also an accredited author herself, having penned feminist music history tome *Revenge of the She-Punks*. After a few back and forths on time zones ahead of a call, I had a cautious response from Goldman explaining that Renee wasn't aware of the book plans which made her reluctant to speak on the subject. The same situation happened a month later when I was directed to long-standing music critic, former A&R director for Columbia, and friend of the band Carol Cooper. Again, I was told that Renee was not on board with the project, and respectfully, Cooper declined to comment.

But then, after a career blighted by exploitation and ill-measured earnings, is it any surprise to find the Scroggins wary of yet another industry type benefiting from the family's hard graft? What started as an aspirational moment of creativity and youthful exuberance drummed up in their teens has become an ongoing battle of royalties and remuneration that the eldest Scroggins' sister is still facing today. Rather than singing the praises of a genre-defying body of work like the band's debut, *Come Away with ESG*, there has been more focus on the group's internal disputes than on their long-standing impact on modern-day music. We need to recognize the musical accomplishments and innovation that countless bands have used to their own advantage (in some cases with little credit). That's why this small nod to the gargantuan talent of a band like ESG feels like a step toward finally repaying some of those debts.

More than ever, music criticism needs to provide a platform to amplify voices that differ from the norm. Having performed as part of a touring band for much of my twenties, I can recall countless times when I was faced with derogatory comments on stage or crude assumptions from shop assistants who clearly felt I had no idea what I was doing in the guitar department. But those biases would have been tenfold for a band of young Black women from the South Bronx like ESG.

The sister collective was by no means the first women of color to pick up the guitar. They needed only to look into the vaults of the works of Memphis Minnie back in the early 1900s or Brazilian guitarist Rosinha de Valença during bossa nova's peak in the 1960s; these women have paved the way for so many contemporary artists today.

But the Scroggins sisters did something that those other artists failed to do. They took their talent and they made it an all-inclusive party. Whether you were at house music's birthplace Chicago or at The Haçienda in Manchester, the Scroggins sisters had you at the beat. As Brian Howe sums up in Paste magazine, "ESG's name is less known than it should be, but its influence runs deep—which is likely why *Come Away with ESG* sounds so shockingly current." The roaming basslines of sing-along opener "Come Away" have gone on to spin similarly golden string sounds for London queer punks Shopping (also strong believers of the disco-not-disco drums), while their spartan arrangements and house music crossover have filled an ample pool of possibility for fellow-primitive Norwich-based noisemakers Sink Ya Teeth.

By selecting *Come Away with ESG*, a body of work that reframed music making for so many as you'll hear throughout these pages, I hope to reposition the spotlight back onto the sisterhood who made it. That's another reason why you won't hear my voice much in these pages. This was always ESG's South Bronx story. This book is here to share the might of such a seismic debut with a wider music-savvy crowd, and, using our two interview times together, I hope to share as much of Renee's experiences in her words or with those who have felt its force in their fingers as they crafted their own songs in the years that followed.

So in a bid to prove ESG's unwavering influence across the ages, I cast the net wider for comment and spoke to some pop heavyweights in the current landscape—the punk prodigies who were also keen to see the group's status shaken up in music history. A paragon like fellow New Yorker Karen O who found her own confidence and autonomy as a South Korean—born songwriter against a backdrop of predominantly male and white bands. Or the new guard of DIY artists like Argentinian punks Las Kellies who, even thirty years on from its release, immediately positioned the band's debut *Come Away with ESG* as the north star to their noise making.

Now, forty years on from that debut and in the wake of the Black Lives Matter movement, the band's first full-length *Come Away with ESG* deserves to be at the center stage of that discussion—the story of how four teenage girls from the Bronx picked up their guitars on Christmas Day and began carving out a space for themselves, with a universal gift in mind, to make people dance. Little did they know that their modest ambition to get the club floors of downtown Manhattan moving would create a seismic shift across the globe, changing the very idea of modern dance music as we know it forever.

1

The South Bronx Story

For a young Renee Scroggins, the Bronx wasn't the cradle of hip hop that it has since become legendary for spawning. Long before the birth of those beats, the borough on the banks of the Harlem River was already boasting a melting pot of musical styles. In the 1920s, Courtlandt Avenue was referred to as "Dutch Broadway," referencing the early German community of the First World War. Twenty years later, the area had embedded itself as "El Condado de la Salsa" after an influx of Puerto Ricans migrated from the island to New York City. And, come the 1950s, the streets were notoriously serving up jazz nights across the blocks as tiny, Black-owned hole-in-the-wall bars like Club 845 hosted revered trumpeter Miles Davies and pianist Herbie Hancock. Over the last thirty years, following the gentrification of the area after the Second World War, the Bronx had become many things, to many people. But for Renee Scroggins, the beating heart of ESG and the eldest of four sisters, the South Bronx was home.

According to *The New York Times*,[1] the New York City Housing Authority (NYCHA) was home to about 500,000 New Yorkers by the 1960s. The Scroggins household was one of those families. Based in the Moore Houses on Jackson Avenue, the two 20-story buildings hosted close to 500 apartments inside. While that might sound like a metropolitan monolith, the two blocks did offer some much-needed green space sidling up alongside St. Mary's Park, one of the six original green zones in the Bronx and the largest of its kind in the South Bronx. From her apartment block window, Renee Scroggins could see kids clambering onto one another's shoulders playing "Johnny the Pony" down on the concrete below. She could hear the sound of guaguancó wafting up from the lawns as resident Puerto Ricans dished out Cuban rumba rhythms on freestanding congas.

It was this fusion of influences from Puerto Rican, Black, Jamaican, and other Afro-Caribbean communities that provided the backdrop to the New York "projects." Brewed up by NYCHA in the 1930s to ease the housing crisis following the Great Depression, the buildings existed across the five boroughs of New York City as an affordable housing option. But it was actually only ten years before that city policy shifted in a bid to promote racial integration within the precincts. *The New York Times* covered the rise in social housing in 1964 after Jesse Gray, a Harlem rent striker, spoke out in a WABC press conference calling for an opening up of "all vacancies to those people in Harlem who need them."[2]

Yet despite the move toward equal application for residents, the need for this type of social housing was far greater than the positions available. In the same *The New York Times* article, Peter Kihiss reported 85,000 applicants for the program a year with only 6,000 vacancies making it impossible to meet demand. Instead, African Americans in urban ghettos were increasingly isolated, and, with mortgage guarantees, the government began subsidizing white communities to abandon urban areas for the leafy suburbs. This conflict conjured up feelings of tension and disparity between the groups that were, ironically, brought together to create a rainbow of diversity on its grounds.

"The South Bronx at one time was a paradise. People sitting on the tenement stoop talking to each other. Everybody knows the name of the police officer that works the beat," explains co-artistic director of the Bronx Music Heritage Center, Bobby Sanabria. The seven-time Grammy-nominated musician grew up in the Melrose Project, just a few blocks away from the Scroggins family in Moore Houses. "The Bronx was a destination for working-class people with middle-class values. They aspired that their kids would go to school and, hopefully, go to college and make it on the next level."[3]

But, by the 1970s, the Big Apple was starting to rot. New York City was rejected for aid by the federal government. Robert Moses's creation of the Cross Bronx Expressway uprooted thousands, displacing communities and fostering white flight (the migration of white people from areas becoming more racially or ethnoculturally diverse). Seven different census tracts in the borough claimed to have lost more than 97 percent of their buildings to fire and abandonment between 1970 and 1980.[4] Thousands of miles across the Atlantic Ocean, on the streets of rural France, locals were even using the neighborhood as slang for a shambolic situation with cries of "Ack, c'est le Bronx!"[5]

The borough's reputation had reached an all-time low. New York wasn't the only city ablaze at that time though;

Detroit was burning following the 1967 riots between Black residents and the Detroit Police department; also Newark was burning after similar race-focused riots, which prompted looting and property destruction to crash through the city. So why did the Bronx become this renowned symbol of urban decay? Fellow co-artistic director and Sanabria's partner, Elena Martinez, believes that there's one particular headline moment that caught the world's attention.

"In 1977, there was a blackout in the World Series and, while millions were watching, the sportscaster Howard Cosell said 'There it is, ladies and gentlemen, the Bronx is burning' but that's legendary,"[6] Martinez says. It's true that Cosell never actually said those words. The scene might've become a defining image of New York at the time, but tapes from that night reveal that that line was never heard over the commentary of the game. But the sixty million people who tuned in to watch the World Series that night did see the blaze ravaging the vacant building on 158th St and Melrose Avenue, only further making the space synonymous with destruction and chaos.

The fires even caught the attention of the Senate at the time as the World Series footage led to a personal visit to the Bronx by President Jimmy Carter in October 1977. Among his stops was Charlotte Street, where Carter declared the now sleepy section of the borough "the worst slum in America" and a symbol of urban blight. A few years later Ronald Reagan, who was running against Carter at the time, also visited the area after addressing the National Urban League Conference in New York in 1980. Four years later and Democratic party nominee, Jesse Jackson, even spent a night in one of the Bronx' famed projects to draw attention to the plight of the poor.

Flick through archive photos of the location at the time and the three-block stretch appears war torn, an apocalyptic site of abandoned buildings, shards of glass, and broken furniture turfed out onto smoldering rubble. "It looks like Dresden after the war," admits Sanabria, downheartedly. "For anybody who's never seen these types of pictures before, you show them and they'll say 'Oh, this must be in Europe' but it's the South Bronx, man."[7]

Back on the streets of the borough—and not doing much to counter that association—there was a huge rise in reported crimes.[8] Many of these are linked by the police to the youth gangs proliferating in the South Bronx. "I would say there are people walking around today that are still alive who should be brought up on murder charges because what they did caused a lot of deaths, a lot of inhumanity and a lot of unnecessary pain,"[9] Sanabria confesses. It wasn't just the gangs causing irreversible damage on the streets though.

A modest tree-lined working class community now boasting cookie-cutter two up, two downs, with black shutters and white facades, Crotona Park's Charlotte Street was a fiery wasteland during the early 1970s as rampant arson gutted the streets of low-income households. Unable to sell their properties, landlords were plotting to burn down their own buildings so they could claim their insurance value. They often hired arsonists, sometimes minors, to torch the buildings for a few dollars, leaving Black and Puerto Rican tenants without a home. On Crimmins Avenue, the same year that the Scroggins sisters would begin forming their family band, newspaper photos portrayed a sole figure wandering down the burnt-out section of the suburb, derelict buildings, looming over him as he passes the carcass of an old Chevrolet Malibu jacked up on bricks and rubble.

Vivien Goldman, author of *Revenge of the She-Punks*, was another musician living in New York at the time (she would later go on to release her *Dirty Washing* EP (extended play record) on the same label as ESG) who heard about these get-rich-quick schemes.

> The landlords were just looking at the bottom line. They had no morality or conscience. RZA from Wu-Tang Clan explained to me that they build projects where more and more people will come up from the South seeking their fortune in the North. Then we have the overcrowding, the drugs, the guns which are pushed to create unrest, to create an underclass, to destabilise the civil rights movement and the Black Panthers.[10]

Goldman's claims ring true with the racial segregation that political activist Jackson was also seeing on the streets as he called for an end to discrimination in the construction trade, arguing that "you can't police poverty. But you can develop people where you live so there's less need for police."[11] For many parents, they were faced with the frightening realization that their children would be faced with one of two choices—"the walking death of narcotics or the violent world of street gangs."[12] For a mother of five young women (an elder sister had already flown the coop), Helen Scroggins was acutely aware that she needed to find another way for the sisters to socialize and express themselves away from the threat of felonies and soporific substances. Renee recalled her mother's determination in the Chicago-based magazine *Venus* and explained how "between the ages of 10 and 14, my mother didn't want us hanging out on the street 'cause a lot of wild things were going on in the South Bronx at the time."[13]

In that sense, the decision to form a band wasn't just a thirteen-year-old Renee's curiosity to learn the bass guitar but the promise of a future outside of the projects. Helen Scroggins wasn't the first parent setting her sights on something more for her offspring. Sanabria also prided himself on listening to his elders, finding a way through the chaos into the limelight. "If anybody is successful, like me, or Sonia Sotomayor (Bronx-born associate justice of the Supreme Court of the United States), it's like we were raised by wolves. It wasn't that our parents gave a shit and wanted us to study. It was persistence and people giving a shit about you."[14] Renee felt similarly buoyed by her mother's hopes for her and her sisters, despite the borough's fabled shortfallings: "Growing up in the projects, my Mom always told us, there is nothing that you can't do."[15]

Despite her optimism for her daughters' budding creative careers, the tension mounting around the South Bronx at the time was palpable. Residents began to feel that this gang mentality was part of a wider sickness of the borough, and by the 1980s, it was said you were "more at risk of criminal violence on NYCHA property than you were in the surrounding neighbourhood."[16] When it came to her clan, Scroggins' mother was determined to keep her family distracted and immersed in a more developmental environment. Renee remembers the juxtaposition vividly. "It was a bad time. It was inspirational as far as if you didn't want to be on those streets, you had to find another way out."[17]

Music became a symbol of hope for them, a place of refuge and resilience against a backdrop of turf territoriality. Inspired by hearing the smooth sounds of her father, John Scroggins, playing the saxophone around the apartment, Renee had already begun performing in the school orchestra and in high school had sung in the school chorus, emulating the choir she and her family often saw on Sundays at church. Inspired by her obvious knack for melody, Helen Scroggins looked to one of her eldest daughter's passions to focus the rest of her crew's creativity. "My mother didn't want us hanging out [on the streets] so we were given a project. She knew I had a love of music, and that my younger sisters would generally fall in line with what I wanted to do, so she got us instruments."[18]

In the winter of 1977, Scroggins recalls the Christmas when she and her sisters came down the stairs to find the musical gifts under the tree. "I have old Super 8 movies, and whenever we do a [ESG] documentary, that will be part of it," she says. With a meagre income, it was a fairly modest setup but it moved the sisters away from their pots and oatmeal boxes in the kitchen and onto the real deal. "I got a bass guitar, Valerie got drums, and Marie got tambourines,"[19] Scroggins continues.

At first, I didn't appreciate what she did for us but, as the years went on, I realised the key sacrifices she made. She was a cook making a salary but she scrimped and saved to get those instruments. She was trying to make sure what happened to my older sister and brothers didn't turn out that way for the rest of us kids.[20]

Evenings in the Scroggins' household were often spent watching variety shows like *Soul!* and *Don Kirshner's Rock Concert*, with live performances from Billy Joel to Black Sabbath. Syndicated series like Kirshner's bridged the gap between the vaudevillian skits of the 1950s and 1960s into the dawn of televising popular music like the BBC's *Disco 2*, the successor to *Colour Me Pop* and the precursor of the more widely applauded *Old Grey Whistle Test* which aired on BBC2 from 1971 to 1988. But it wasn't just Kirsner's shows that sparked the Scroggins sisters' desire to perform.

Despite only being thirteen years old at the time, Renee Scroggins remembers their excitement at seeing family groups like the Jackson brothers performing in their own version of the notorious variety show format. "We saw The Jackson 5 [and] at that particular time, they were kids and that gave you the inspiration even as kids you can get out there and do it."[21] *The Jacksons* aired between 1976 and 1977 after running for 12 episodes and featured all the Jackson siblings aside from Jermaine Jackson who was already signed to Motown at the time. It was the first variety show where the entire cast was from an African American family.

Propelled by their fellow singing sibling troupe, the Scroggins sisters set about designing their own brand as performers. They went through a number of name changes before finally settling on ESG. "E" stood for emerald, Valerie's birthstone; "S" stood for sapphire, Renee's birthstone; and the birthstone of neither Deborah nor Marie was garnet, but instead, the "G" marked their ambition as a band—the road to a gold record. They added percussionist Tito Libran to the lineup, and ESG was born. The sisters quickly began familiarizing themselves with simple chord structures and melodies from well-known songs but soon realized that the glitz of the variety shows was hard to drum up from their bedrooms. "Watching it on TV was easier than the reality, you had to focus! We first attempted to play cover songs. My favourite was (The Rolling Stones') 'Satisfaction' but that was horrible so I quickly realised that if I wrote my own songs nobody would know if we messed up,"[22] recalls Renee Scroggins.

Alongside their Rolling Stones repertoire, the young performers wove in versions of Chaka Khan and her funk band, Rufus, clearly already harboring an appetite for a hybrid mix of rhythms. Rehearsals would culminate in a Friday night music review with the band's biggest fan and looming critic, Helen Scroggins. "What I liked about our Mum was she didn't tell us we were terrible, she would just say 'It needs a little more work.' She was very encouraging,"[23] Scroggins recollects fondly.

Fresh from their Friday night rehearsals, their mother started entering her daughters into talent shows and local contests. It was during one such event that a chance encounter would set ESG's trajectory whirring. The competition's judging panel was streets more credible than the reality shows that have since come to plague our TVs, like high-waisted honcho Simon Cowell's *Popstars* or saying hello to Lionel Richie again around the judges' panel of *American Idol*, as households across the country vote for their favorite act.

Instead, the CBS Records—sponsored show in Manhattan's Music Building saw Ed Bahlman of 99 Records and Jim Farah of notorious disco club Peppermint Lounge (the space that was the launchpad for the global Twist craze in the early 1960s) making the final call.

Despite not even placing in the contest, Bahlman was intrigued by this brood of siblings from the South Bronx and offered to be the band's manager and soundman, as Renee Scroggins remembers.

> They said they're looking for new music and, at the end of it, Ed just took my number and he rings me up and he says: 'I'm doing something down in Manhattan, would you guys be interested in playing?' and he booked us our first professional gig, where we made a whopping and exciting $150. I still have that actual receipt—I will keep that forever![24]

Under Bahlman's lead, ESG landed their first paying gig at Mechanics' Hall at a show called *Popfront*. The vast venue on Broadway now boasts five function rooms including The Great Hall which can host a symphony orchestra or fundraising gala for its esteemed clientele. But for ESG, the venue was simply a chance to dust off their early setlist and hit the club scene of the city. The Scroggin sisters quickly began lining up shows across New York with their characteristic minimalist funk forays coolly lending themselves to the burgeoning postpunk and newly established no-wave scene of the early 1980s.

A reaction against the new-wave sensibilities of their pop-leaning peers like Blondie, Talking Heads, and The Velvet

Underground, "no wave" channeled noise, dissonance, and atonality. Experimental by nature, no wave left behind any fixed style or genre much like ESG, who in their forty-plus years on the music scene refused to be pigeonholed into a particular sound or style. They were indie drifters surfing somewhere between New York with its signature melding of musical styles and equally embraced by Manchester's post-punk movement that was happening around the same time over on British shores (you'll often find me leaning on both reference points depending on the track in question).

Forming in late 1970s New York, their music quickly became pegged in the no-wave scene thanks to its mash up of disparate styles, from their improvisational skills straight out of the Latino communities in Moore Houses to their stripped-back, bass-heavy beats, rich in repetitive rhythms. The term "no wave" is rumored to be a part satiric wordplay on the then-popular New Wave genre coined by American singer and poet Lydia Lunch (although Sonic Youth founder Thurston Moore also claims to have seen the phrase graffitied on the walls of hallowed New York City club, CBGBs).

Regardless of its roots though, no wave's significance lies in its embodiment of a particular moment in New York's artistic history where a jaded, post-Vietnam underground fostered a cadre of writers, performers, and artists like pop purveyor Keith Haring, Nuyorican neo-expressionist Jean Michel Basquiat, and avant-garde multimedia creative and Lou Reed's longtime partner Laurie Anderson. For *Village Voice* writer Steve Anderson, the no-wave scene was pivotal in proceedings referring to the period as "New York's last stylistically cohesive avant-rock movement." Yet for such a hallowed era, and much like ESG's first label 99 Records, no wave's output was fairly modest. But its impact on modern-day music was mighty.

At the same time, miles away from Manhattan in the streets of Manchester, another dissonant revolution was bubbling in working-class England. Punk indebted acts like shapeshifting noisemakers The Fall, surly Salford trio Joy Division, and stylistically perverse A Certain Ratio were also drawing on a disparate range of influences across music and modern art. The last group shared Renee Scroggins and her sisters' passion for fusing together elements of funk, jazz, postpunk, and noise into their unique sprawling soundscapes. It's possibly not surprising to hear then that A Certain Ratio's label boss at the time, the late great Tony Wilson of British indie label Factory Records, saw an opportunity for the band to head to New York and record their first album over there, capturing that truly authentic no-wave flavor. His plan worked. 1980s 12" "Blown Away" is supercharged with dynamic drum fills and even rogue snatches of bird song that could have been gleaned straight from the greenery of St. Mary's Park. The same year the band recorded their debut studio album with acclaimed producer, and Tony Wilson's original partner at Factory Records, Martin Hannett at Eastern Artists Recording Studio (E.A.R.S) in East Orange, New Jersey.

In between laying down their first full length, Wilson wanted the band in the thick of the live scene, booking them shows to perform across Chicago, Boston, and downtown New York. The last show saw the unassuming Manchester fivesome headlining at a short-lived art nightclub alongside a fresh-faced ESG, as guitarist and producer of the band Martin Moscrop recounted to Drowned in Sound back in 2009: "[It] was a fantastic experience for five young Manchester lads. The first gig we played was at Tier 3—a small venue with a brand new New York band, ESG supporting."[25] (In subsequent years, A Certain Ratio would go on to find themselves on the bill with quite a few notable names in the city, even sharing the stage with a young Madonna at dancefloor heaven Danceteria in the winter of 1982!)

Meanwhile, backstage at Tier 3, the Scroggins sisters pose for a photo in front of peeling archive show posters that crudely line the walls, all decked out in similarly glitzy blouses and dark crushed velvet. It's a rare photo moment capturing the full Scroggins family. Their father John stares directly at the camera, hands on his hips. Renee elevated with the aid of a chair, beams from the back row, one hand placed on each of her parents' shoulders. Their mother Helen is in the heart of the fold looking off to the side, a nervous authority figure as most of the band is all still technically too young to frequent these types of clubs alone. The rest of the group smiles serenely at the camera with little knowledge that their world is about to change irrevocably.

After their set that night, Tony Wilson approached the band about making a record, and in Renee Scroggins's mind, it was that moment when things really started to escalate.

When I met Tony Wilson that was when ESG really got to play. Ed [Bahlman] had been managing us for a year and he hadn't really done anything. He had put out a vinyl by Bush Tetras and I asked him and he was like "yeah, yeah,

yeah." It wasn't until Tony Wilson was really interested that we decided to do something with them.[26]

A week later, ESG—like so many of their postpunk peers—also headed into the studio with Martin Hannett to put together a three-track single for release in the UK— the deal with Bahlman? (Legend has it that Hannett was only available because Joy Division had booked studio time that had to be cancelled following Ian Curtis's suicide.[27]) In return, 99 Records took the three Factory songs and added in three live tracks from the band's performance at Hurrah in December 1980 to make a split studio/live 12-inch EP for the United States. Released in mid-February 1981, *ESG* built on the diverse sounds that surrounded the sisters growing up to create eighteen minutes of infectious grooves and economical funk, mostly percussion and bass but with vital contributions from the band's unofficial mouthpiece/leader 21-year-old Renee Scroggins.

"You're No Good" slays a self-fulfilled lover with clattering congas straight from Renee's memories of those balmy summer nights in Moore Houses. "I remember opening our windows and hearing Latin music. They would be playing congas and using coke bottles instead of cowbells,"[28] she shared in an interview together in 2017. While the bass line on "Moody" conjures up a visible shoulder shuffle that James Brown would be proud of, in fact, the Godfather of Soul was one of the Scroggins sisters' biggest influences, especially when it came to those drum and bass-heavy arrangements in their songwriting. "I used to love when James Brown would 'take it to the bridge,' and he'd take away the horns and it would be just bass and drums," Renee reflected on the forefather of funk. "I thought, 'What if we made a whole song that sounded like that bridge?'"[29]

What it sounded like was sparse, its roots roaming with Renee's bass rhythms and that propellant percussion. Listening to the sisters' polyrhythms proudly morphing from drum and bass beats to a more proto punk pace, it's easy to hear the influence on a legion of new-wave and postpunk bands that would follow. That, after all, is the brilliance of a band like ESG—the ability to transcend preexisting genres and scenes. You're just as likely to find them rubbing shoulders with both The Clash and Grandmaster Flash in the same evening. It was actually the former who invited a swathe of young Black artists including ESG, Bad Brains, and the Furious Five to support them during their weeklong residency at New York's Bond's International Casino in the early summer of 1981.[30]

The live flip side to the self-titled EP is possibly less well-known than the Factory-focused Aside. But "Earn It" still showcases the band's trademark clout and Spartan sound with Renee Scroggins laying out the lessons she was no doubt raised on, as she sings, "There ain't nothing in this life that's free / If you want some of that green money / You have to do something called work, you see / If you want some of that green money / You have to earn it." The toppling bass lines and drum shuffles head straight into "Hey" with an intro that's as tight as the opening snare slaps of George Harrison's pop belter "I've Got My Mind Set On You." Only rather than wading into some quirky 1980s singalong, the track finds Renee Scroggins experimenting with some low, slow slides on the guitar and a rainfall of rhythm sticks (Ian Dury would be proud) before descending into the band's fist-pumping theme tune as they chant "ESG" to close.

It's a worthy fanfare. In an interview with ABC Radio from the early 1980s,[31] Bahlman shared that the release was the most commercially successful release to come out on 99 (alongside the Bush Tetras single) with the added international distribution from Factory Records. So much so that by the summer of 1981, the label had to make a second pressing of the release. The record's most enduring legacy, however, would come with its later (and unintentional) entrance into the hip hop era. An instrumental number structured around the sound of a piercing strain of guitar reverb, "UFO" didn't exactly come across as your go-to single choice, but, to Renee Scroggins, that was never really the intention. "We played it as we always meant it to be which is it's a song about aliens—it was about aliens landing in the middle of a province."[32]

The story goes that during their first recording session with Hannett, ESG hadn't planned on even recording the track. But after laying down both "You're No Good" and "Moody," Hannett explained the tape was still rolling if they wanted to do another song. "I said, 'Yeah UFO'!" begins Renee Scroggins. "It's funny because my sisters hated 'UFO' at first because when we used to play it, it would start and the audience would look at us like, 'What the hell is that?'" But I said, "I love 'UFO', this is my song! If it wasn't for the fact that there were only three minutes of tape left, 'UFO' might never have been on that first Factory EP."[33]

What they didn't know at the time though was that thanks to that chance take in the recording booth, the track would go onto become one of the most sampled songs ever in hip hop history. So while many music fans might not have heard of ESG, their legacy rings out across tracks from as far-reaching as Notorious BIG to The Prodigy. As Tim O'Neil states in PopMatters, "It's pretty much impossible to imagine about half of the dance music or hip hop that exists today ever having been created without the influence of the Scroggins sisters."[34]

What makes the legacy of ESG so special is the unassuming but seismic impact the sisters had on countless musical genres across the ages; because it wasn't just "UFO" that made it onto turntables across the United States. In underground clubs of Chicago and New York in the late 1970s, house music origins were beginning to take root. DJs were experimenting with new ways of mixing their sets to keep people dancing, and remixing techniques gave new life to dance music in the dying disco era.

The term "house music" was coined in Chicago, the place believed to have birthed the genre. And it was here that the EP's other sample hit, "Moody," made it onto Chip E.'s—the Godfather of house music—record deck using the song's bassline for his 1985 single "Like This." Not only did the Scroggins sisters define their own fresh sounds against the backdrop of New York's new-wave scene but their riffs went onto shape some of the biggest songs in modern dance music. After all, surely that's the beauty of such an original sound? O'Neil agrees: "At the risk of sounding condescending, ESG have carved out their unique place in music history by dint of being an anomaly."[35]

While the family might have grown up against a backdrop of dilapidated buildings and scorched road surfaces, this setting only forged their connection closer together as a family. Helen Scroggins made sure to surround the sisters with early encouragement and loving support in those early days, as fellow 99 Records roster member Vivien Goldman attests: "Their mother was a heroine to have that vision with nobody around them as a role model."[36] With the myriad of musical references and its own innovative idea of song structures and subjects (!), *ESG* artfully avoids pigeon holing. For Scroggins, the band's vision—much like their lyrics—have remained straight from the shoulder.

"The only thing I've always said to people is that ESG's music makes you want to dance. Other than that, I don't like to put us in a genre or a box. We are ourselves."[37] The problem being, of course, much like the subject matter of their extraterrestrial single, in some cases their talent is unidentifiable in the record credits. But if the South Bronx had taught this sisterhood anything, it was that you needed to be tough and you needed to state your territory. The sound of that is no clearer than on the band's full-length debut *Come Away with ESG*.

2

From Downtown Manhattan to Up North Manchester: Come Away with ESG

In its six-year existence, 99 Records put out just twenty-three releases, but its contribution to the New York music scene (and beyond) cannot be overestimated. Many of its artists went on to have an immeasurable impact on some of the most iconic rock bands in history (see Sonic Youth's endless appreciation for avant-garde composer Glenn Branca). Even with its instant impact though, the label—founded by born and bred Brooklynite Ed Bahlman—didn't begin conventionally. Instead, what went on to be the fabled shop front of the label began life as a punk clothing and accessories store, a few blocks south of Washington Square Park.

99 Macdougal Street was run by British clothes designer Gina Franklyn, who moved to New York in 1970 and incidentally became the first person in the United States to import Doc Martens among its accessory racks. The store sat below ground—much like the artists Bahlman would go on to support and showcase. Originally visiting the store as a customer, Bahlman and Franklyn hit it off and soon began

dating. The music aficionado became a regular behind the counter, pitching in with sales shifts, and it was during that time he managed to sneak his first few singles onto the shelves. Inspired by meetings with UK postpunk instigator Richard Boon, band manager of The Buzzcocks and boss of the New Hormones label, Bahlman decided to try his hand in the business too. And with his niche knowledge of both the reggae and rock scene alongside Franklyn's Brit-based connections, 99 Records soon became *the* place to shop for postpunk pioneers. Early 99 recording artist Glenn Branca even dubbed the space a "collector's store."

Fellow label alumna Vivien Goldman can still see the shop's spot on the square as a huge contributing factor to 99 Records' pivotal role in the downtown music scene of the early 1980s, as she recalls. "That location was the epicenter through gentrified streets full of little artisans and Mom + Pop stores with very cheap rents for the artists."[1] Perhaps, unsurprisingly, considering its owners, the store's origin story drew parallels to two UK institutions: The first, Vivienne Westwood's SEX store, which was active on the renowned King's Road in London between 1974 and 1976, and the second, following Bahlman's involvement, was Rough Trade (Geoff Travis opened his first flagship shop off Ladbroke Grove in 1978). But there was another more imminent rival looming large: Sp. Bleecker Bob's, the iconic Greenwich Village record store, existed right around the corner on Third Street.

The vinyl mecca was forever immortalized in a 1993 episode of Seinfeld when Kramer and Newman try (and ultimately) fail to sell their used records there, and it's also where a customer named Patti Smith met record salesman Lenny Kaye and invited him to accompany her on the guitar at a poetry reading. Four decades later, Kaye is still accompanying Smith to this day. Sp. Bleecker Bob's was rooted in the idiosyncratic culture of Greenwich Village, but when 99 Records opened, artists and creatives were quick to brush off the bohemian approach of Bob for Bahlman's more modern approach. Sonic Youth's Thurston Moore was an early shopper at the newly established store effusively stating, "99 Records opened up and was way hipper than Sp. Bleecker Bob's."[2]

It was an interesting time in the Big Apple, with the city at a musical crossroads: The lively disco scene that ran through the 1970s was fading (there were only so many times Bianca Jagger could mount a white pony inside Studio 54), and the punk scene propelled by CBGBs was quickly turning mainstream. Even rap was moving away from the block parties of the Bronx and into swanky recording studios. Naturally, the no-wave movement felt like the perfect anecdote to this major label talent show. Set against this backdrop, not only did 99 Records become one of the central gathering points for indie types in New York's underground music scene but Bahlman also ended up releasing a fair chunk of the artists in question.

Avant-garde musician and composer Glenn Branca's *Lesson No.1* celebrated a number of firsts for the label: Branca's debut 12" release and the inaugural record that Bahlman himself put out in 1980 on the freshly founded 99 Records. The track is eight minutes of Branca's (now notorious) sprawling guitars, alternate tunings, and a violin weaving through it all in a frenzy. But even with such a novel approach to instrumentation, the guitarist was very aware of how his experimental leanings had gone on to be refined by a whole new generation of artists: "Sonic Youth gave [people] what I had, but sugar-coated it. They knew I'd come up with all these incredibly cool sounds that could be used in the context of a rock song. At the time I wasn't going to do that."[3]

Another debut came from original dance punks, Bush Tetras, who released *Too Many Creeps* 7" on 99 Records the same year. In *Revenge of the She-Punks*, Vivien Goldman's fascinating look into feminist music history, the NYU professor and fellow 99 Records artist recounts a story about the band lending their gear at a local show to a very young ESG. Unlike the Scroggins siblings, Bush Tetras were entrenched in the downtown music scene. With guitarist Pat Place already famed for his founding role of no-wave act The Contortions, the group quickly began receiving significant airplay on WNEW-FM and the New York dance club circuit (a given thanks to those funky bass lines). Reflecting on forty years of the band with *Louder Than War* in 2020, drummer Dee Pop explained the fortuitous run-in with Bahlman that led to the band's signing.

Me and my mother went to Hunter College on 68th Street to see a reggae group, Black Uhuru. It was their first show in New York—I have a very cool mom. In the middle of the show, someone took out a gun and started shooting. Everyone ran out onto Lexington Avenue and started hiding behind cars. Me and my mother are behind this car, and Ed and Gina were by the car as well. We're all like, underneath this car, and my mother says to Ed, "he's got a great new band! You should sign them!" And the next week Bush Tetras were on 99.[4]

Legend goes that the band recorded the one-off 45" with equipment belonging to John Travolta's brother who was trying to ride the hype of his sibling's multiplying fame.

The same year, all-female no wavers Y Pants dished out their *Little Music* EP under Bahlman's guidance which was also recorded by fellow 99 label buddy Glenn Branca. The trio, made up of photographer/musician Barbara Ess, visual artist Virginia Piersol, and filmmaker Gail Vachon, took the idea of lo-fi to new extremes plugging in their novel tiny instruments into regular-sized amplifiers to pen quirky numbers about the perils of laundry day ("Favourite Sweater") and phone frustrations ("Off the Hook"). The band's feminist poetics and inventive instrumentation made them a hit in Manhattan's art gallery scene.

Unlike their 99 Records peers though, Renee Scroggins and her sisters weren't known on the New York City circuit and were a bit of a punt from Bahlman. Emboldened after spotting the siblings at that CBS Records–sponsored show, the Brooklynite began booking gigs for the band including their first headline slot at one of New York's first large-scale dance clubs, Hurrah. In a 99 Records press release from the time, the label heralded the band's "deceptively simple, direct funk" and explains how it "continues to break new ground while breaking in ever-larger audiences." As to be expected from the early EP release, ESG were celebrated for their "word-defying sound" although the media had to try. Dean of American Rock Critics, Robert Christgau, is quoted on the release as calling the group "minimalist salsa" and "bare-boned funk" (although he would later go on to call them "overrated dance-oriented rock" in *The Village Voice*).[5]

Opening for ESG at Hurrah that night were Liquid Liquid, a dub-fused rhythm section/band that, despite having performed around Manhattan for the last year, made their first major debut at the show with the press release promising "a night of pioneer rhythms." The same could be said for Liquid Liquid's self-titled EP which had landed earlier that season. Six months on, though, rather than the local musicians he'd planted roots with, Bahlman began releasing a string of tracks by mostly British acts whose sound fit in with his increasingly more dub and reggae-focused tastes. The first of these was Vivien Goldman who began her career as a journalist before becoming a PR officer at Atlantic Records and then Island Records, famously working with Bob Marley. Impressed with her past record in reggae, Bahlman was immediately intrigued when Goldman headed over to the United States with her *Dirty Washing* EP and producer John Lydon (yes, the very same one from the Sex Pistols) looking to grow stateside.

Goldman had heard of Bahlman and the burgeoning business that he and Franklyn had set up in Greenwich Village and was certain he was the guy to distribute the record in New York City. "I took it around to him. I literally went in and played him the tape. He was there serving in the shop," she shares, animatedly. "I can't remember what format I had it on, whether it was a cassette or an early pressing or something. But I just played it for him and he said, 'Oh yeah, let's do a deal.' So I said, 'Perfect. Go for it.'"[6]

For Goldman, Bahlman's indie enterprise offered up an alternative to the hegemony of the multinationals, and she admits to finding his approach refreshing, particularly around the presumed prime of a female artist at the time. "There were still those restrictive, reductive contracts and the way especially a woman should be. I was already at that top edge because I was in my early thirties so that was the appeal. [99 Records] were doing interesting things."[7] She also recalls Bahlman working "very autonomously," much like Rough Trade's Geoff Travis whose left-wing label had already made huge waves in the UK music scene. After releasing a string of successful singles from the Monochrome Set, Subway Sect, and Kleenex, Rough Trade's first full-length album, *Inflammable Material*, by Stiff Little Fingers, reached number 14 on the charts and became the first independently released album to sell over 100,000 copies in the UK.

While 99 Records' shop didn't boast quite the same socializing space as Rough Trade, where bands and punters alike could hang out, Goldman did run into the Scroggins siblings a number of times at 99 Macdougal Street. The distinct disparity between the new downtown scene and ESG's multicultural upbringing in the Bronx was instantly clear to her. "They were probably in slightly alien territory because there weren't many people like them in the vicinity of the bohemian studenty, punky West Village. That scene was fairly homogeneously white at the time."[8] But while young in years (the sisters ranged from sixteen to twenty-three years in age at this stage), ESG was far from naive when it came to running the band.

"The thing about [ESG] which I found so admirable and really inspiring was that they were such self-starters," explains Goldman.

I admire people who really succeed in inventing their own reality, nothing to do with what was dictated for them or the little box they were assigned to at birth but who are really working from the gut. They completely struck an original path. It's very, very rarely that you can call anything truly original. Aristotle said, 'There was nothing new under the sun' and that's still correct. But in the case of ESG, even Aristotle would say 'these young ladies are different.[9]

The Scroggins sisters' innovative take on the modern dance funk they dished out was certainly a contributing factor to Factory Records' founder Tony Wilson's decision to fly the band over to open up at the hallowed The Haçienda launch party in May 1982. Five years after its inception, between broadcaster Wilson and actor Alan Erasmus, the Manchester-based label was scaling up, and they tasked British designer Ben Kelly with transforming the Factory aesthetic into a three-dimensional space. When launch night came, the paint was still wet and the sound system was yet to be overhauled.

Enter South Bronx siblings, ESG, in and among the scaffolding and ropey staging, a moment that sticks clearly in Renee Scroggins's mind. "When we turned up, they hadn't even finished building the venue. There was sawdust everywhere, it was killing my allergies!"[10] she jokes. An iconic space in the Manchester music scene wasn't the only thing being birthed that night though, as the elder Scroggins sister performed at the opening party pregnant with her daughter Nicole. She'd also perform later that year at the infamous

New York discotheque Paradise Garage eight months pregnant explaining to Drowned in Sound how the band would "never let being women stop us from doing things. As a matter of fact, when I gave birth to my daughter, three days later I was on stage in Pasadena, California, opening for PiL."[11] No one could ever call the Scroggins sisters work shy.

While bandleader Renee was growing her own family name, Wilson and Erasmus were ushering in straight-laced looking youths in plain tees and open shirt jackets into their fledgling homestead. As the crowds stood chugging tankards of cheap beer at the bar, northern comedian Bernard Manning entered the space as a compere, booked by Wilson, only to immediately condemn the bleak setting and walk straight back out. "I've played some fucking shitholes in my time but this beats the lot of them."[12] With such an eclectic welcome party (and if Alan Partridge's fabled performance of the label owner is anything to go by in *24 Hour Party People*), it's clear that Wilson prided himself on eccentric choices. Why else would he have flown out a relatively unknown South Bronx sister troupe for the evening's opening act?

Cofounder of Joy Division (arguably Factory Records' most famous recording artist) and later New Order, Peter Hook has since become a custodian to the iconic Manchester monolith. Even with his years of commitment (and financial backing to the project), though, Hook struggled to understand the business decision, especially with such a lukewarm response from the crowd. "Nobody knew who they were so it was a bonkers thing to do. In many ways, the gesture was wasted because nobody seemed to give a fuck about these kids playing. They didn't have a banner saying they were from New York and as it was the opening night, they didn't seem to get much of a reception."[13]

For Renee and her sisters, it was business as usual though as they pulled together the set list for their inaugural UK show. But the performance went on to forge a fierce and loyal relationship between the Scroggins clan and the Manchester and Manhattan music scenes, spurred on by Wilson at the helm, in Hook's opinion.

> He really had a thing about New York [and] a fascination with the place. He took A Certain Ratio to record not only their first LP in New York but also their second. It's not like 'Ratio sounded very New York but Tony had a massive passion [for the city]. For him, in bringing ESG to Manchester, he wasn't taking Manchester to New York, he was bringing New York to Manchester.[14]

It would've been easy for this connection to have come together through the bustling scenes of underground London, but instead, it was this Northern city rapidly on the rise that found itself like a punk pen pal. That burgeoning bond was only spurred on by Wilson who ambitiously began looking at ways to cross-pollinate his recording artists into stateside scenarios, as Hook continues, "When we [New Order] went over, Tony was already there with A Certain Radio building this bridge from Manchester to New York. He had us record the second version of *Ceremony* in a New Jersey studio and it looked like he was trying to, with Ruth Polsky, build a bridge between the cities."[15]

But Wilson wasn't just making a name for Manhattan's downtown up north, his vision for The Haçienda's physical presence also acted as the catalyst for Manchester's regeneration. As designer Ben Kelley told *The Vinyl Factory* in 2017, this cathedral-like space catered for something beyond the current nightlife scene up there. "People didn't have anywhere else to go. There were traditional pubs, a few Peter Stringfellow–type places with mirror balls and flocked wallpaper or there were shitty, filthy basements."[16] Likewise, Hook remains proud of the alternative hub The Haçienda became and its earnest roots:

> It was a great combination of a group using their success to invest in Manchester [but it was also] about philanthropy. It wasn't about making money out of people. It was about helping people to have a meeting place. The Hacienda gave this scene a venue. It was like a youth club for adults. It was for the misfits, people who didn't fit into the norm.[17]

Perhaps, that's why ESG felt so welcomed by UK fans and promoters (and do to this day) because their band and musical offerings have never followed the straight and narrow. There was something of an unspoken union between Renee Scroggins and Tony Wilson, and he remains an important lightning rod in the band's early successes as she attests: "One of the biggest misconceptions is that 99 put out our records first. No, Factory did."[18]

Despite its seismic significance in Factory Records' discography, it's not well documented that ESG was actually one of the first American acts to sign to the label. They were also one of the only signings to produce a single release before moving on (the other notably was O.M.D with 7" "Electricity" in 1979 before releasing their debut on Dindisc) using the label as a jumping-off point to a larger record company deal. This setup was an early part of what Tony Wilson wanted for Factory[19].

Hook knew all about Wilson's vision, even if he notes that it was somewhat larger than he and cofounder Erasmus ever really anticipated!

> Tony's thing, both with The Hacienda and Factory Records, was that he never envisaged the scale of what he was creating. He didn't realise he was going to change the world with one band [or] change the world of clubbing with The Hacienda. To think The Hacienda has now become some cultural staple is again a huge compliment to the culture that was created.[20]

From debut UK performances to laying down their debut record, it was also around this time that ESG headed into Radio Music City Hall to record *Come Away with ESG*. The recording studio was a surprisingly traditional setup for such a forward-thinking band with 2" tape reel-to-reel recording and an array of percussion instruments flanking the walls alongside the in-studio piano. Now an entertainment venue renowned as "The Showplace of the Nation," the space is located just behind Times Square in New York. Its cheery neon marquee sign wraps around the front of the building like an old school casino front. This was a proper bright light, big city moment for the Scroggins sisters.

Come Away with ESG remains a groundbreaking stylistic record showcasing the band's (now) signature stripped-down, bottom-heavy sound. Of course, the sister troupe wasn't thinking of such accolades though when they were jamming out sounds together in their bedrooms of the Bronx. They were just looking to make some no-frills fun, dance party beats, and their debut delivers with aplomb on that front. The thing that makes ESG such an influential act to this day is the timeless nature of their songwriting skills. The fact that *Come Away with ESG* sounds so current is testament to its wide-reaching and undeniable impact on modern dance music today and the reams of outfits its primitive sounds have gone on to influence (think LCD Soundsystem right through to more recent queer punks Shopping). Because, despite their lack of wider international fame, ESG remains more influential to this day than most of their no-wave peers.

Their debut is an amalgamation of earlier recordings from studio time with Martin Hannett alongside a suite of new tracks, but even some of those snatch from their previous sessions. Title track and opener "Come Away" channels the same schoolyard chants of early EP B-side "Hey!" as the sisters playfully retort "Oh yeah!" to Renee's offer to "Come and go away with me / We'll have a good time," setting us up for the riot of fun ahead in the rest of the LP (long player record). Valerie Scroggins's primitive disco-not-disco drums are the driving force alongside a cheeky appearance of the cabasa for the metallic shoulder shuffle sound most commonly found in bossa nova pieces.

"Dance" makes a return appearance from 1982's *ESG Says Dance to The Beat of ESG*, bringing an element of Motown magic with a driving bass line that could easily rank against Motown messiahs The Commodores. Fitting really, given that both bands have a shared mission to its central refrain—encouraging us all to bust a move on the dancefloor.

But rather than slick vocal lines, the Scroggins round up a more playful tone with handclaps and whooping hysteria that glides straight into the fellow bass-led brilliance of "You Make No Sense" and those timely rhythm sticks of their earlier EP recordings, as Renee puts a deceiving love affair in its place as she delivers coolly, "You make no sense at all / Why do you lie, boy?"

Instrumental "Chistelle" (named after drummer Valerie Scroggins's new-born daughter at the time) has leanings of fellow 99 Records artist Glenna Branca in its experimental soundscape, introducing more angular lead guitar lines that furrow through the clattering percussion, stop-start cymbals, and an almost rise and fall of sea waves crashing around in your cans. "About You" introduces some hi-frequency 90s synths among the call of the cowbell and Renee's knowing vocal take as she assures us "I know all about you." "Tiny Sticks" is another instrumental riot of rhythms complete with sadly lesser-used vibraslap, and "It's Alright" welcomes dual vocals between Renee and Marie alongside some cantering congas and a self-reassurance that things will work out okay.

A mainstay on BBC Radio 6 Music, the penultimate track "The Beat" feels like an appropriate anthem for a group like ESG as Renee reflects knowingly how "it moves your feet, yeah / How it makes you dance yeah" over percussionist Tito Libran's welcomes return of that rattlesnake slink of that Latin-fused cabasa. While closer, "My Love for You" is like the forbearing funk mother of Red Hot Chilli Peppers' 1996 release, "Rollercoaster of Love" as the group sing how their love goes up, down, and round above some seamlessly flanged cymbal splashes and those timely rhythm sticks keeping time in-between Valerie Scroggins's tom-rich drum fills.

Surprisingly, given its reception in the New York club scene, "UFO" (from their earlier self-titled EP) doesn't make the final cut for the debut. But a cosmic counterpoint exists instead in a novel reworking of "Moody—Spaced Out," which boasts all the analogue oscillators of your average 80s synth band. Some critics might argue that *Come Away with ESG*, with its explorative instrumentals and repeated vocal refrains, presents itself as overly monotonous, but there's something recognizable in the rise and falls of the rhythms that offer up a sense of release. It's disco diva hedonism for a new age. The tracks feel familiar on first listen as if you've known them all along; a unifying sound that transcends decades and genres making it impossible not to move. It becomes a tribal response. This is a family affair, after all.

Through their Haçienda performances and Factory Records release, ESG had been embraced by the UK punk scene as their international touring cousins and into the clubs of New York with their close label peers. But in and among the wave of other righteous female figures making their mark on the music scene at the time, like their intergalactic single release "UFO," the Scroggins sisters remained their own entity. As fellow 99 Records artist, Vivian Goldman articulates, "They weren't Alpha roaring girls like Ari [Up, The Slits] or even Poly [Styrene, X-Ray Spex]. There were no other girls like them. They'd come down from their Projects which were far more violent than the East Village that they were visiting. They were coming from another planet."[21]

And for young girls of that age, even with all of its affluence and artistic community, Manhattan held a darker side. Ironic really, given Helen Scroggins's hope for her daughters was to move away from the fiery flames of the Bronx. Instead, the Scroggins sisters were faced with the corruption of shady music types. Goldman draws the parallels vividly. "They were moving from an environment with one source of overt hostility to another environment that purported to be a lot freer but actually had almost more serious dangers. Unless they were caught in the crossfire, they were among family. But here, the people who were supposed to be working with them were shafting them, shooting them with contracts."[22]

Only with 99 Records, falling under paperwork wasn't really the issue. Many of the label's original releases will fetch a fair few pounds on Discogs as the original rights remain with Bahlman who has notoriously removed himself from the music industry entirely. As Tim Ross reported in his comprehensive look into the 99 Records story for *The Vinyl Factory*, "Bahlman has refused to give up any of the master tapes for any monetary price, thus infuriating many of the 99 artists who have repeatedly tried to get their out-of-print recordings reissued on other labels."[23]

For Scroggins and her sisters this meant that royalties quickly became a rights issue. *Come Away with ESG* follows suit with an artist's traditional trajectory today. You release a handful of singles and EPs and then some of those very same tracks will most likely make it onto your debut record. But while the early demos remain in Renee Scroggins's hands, the re-records of tracks like "Moody" and "Dance" are held by Bahlman's unclenching grasp.

Penalized by their own success, 99 Records distribution of the debut made it one of the label's most commercially successful records to date, so when it came to DJs rifling through the racks, it's likely the track they'd stumble upon to use in the mix was Bahlman's. In the years that followed, the Scroggins sisters' only chance of recouping funds was instead tied up in timely reissues and anniversary compilations. (See FIRE Record's fortieth-anniversary issue of *Come Away with ESG* from 2018 and *The South Bronx Story* compilation in 2002 from London-based multigenre label Soul Jazz Records.)

Back in early 1980s New York, after their initial string of releases with the label, things with 99 Records seemed to go from bad to worse. Bahlman eventually decided to leave the scene and McDougall Street, entirely. Speaking with Goldman, she seemed curious about a wider issue that might have been hanging over Bahlman and his business and how that could have led to such a swift exit: "I used to hear that Ed had had Mafia threats, it had all become too much and he'd just gone underground. The location, I'd lived there and I'd had a Mafia brush myself where I took their advice and did what they said," she recalls stoically. "It was normal to have a Mafia brush and shut up shop if you couldn't deal. But he also relied on everybody's laziness. I was lucky because I owned my masters."[24]

Coming over from the UK with her Laundrette EP in tow, Goldman was a very different proposition to ESG. She had already self-released the record via her own label Window (the parent label was that of her pal Geoff Travis's Rough Trade), and so when Goldman approached Bahlman that day on McDougall Street, the deal was purely for distribution in a bid to get her in front of a wider US audience.

All of this to say that in those days it was clear that contracts weren't necessarily a given. Bands like ESG were propositioned during a talent show; Bush Tetras crouched behind a car during a shoot-out. Renee too remembers the loose arrangement of that period of time in the music industry: "He didn't sign us. It's so funny with labels like 99 Records and Factory Records. There were no contracts, it was just a verbal thing."[25] The problem with that, of course, was longevity. A recording artist no longer had the right to reissue or distribute their early works, some of which were arguably the defining moments of their career. This also explains why many artists, including ESG, have gone on to reissue through British labels.

Goldman continues to reflect on the underbelly of Bahlman. "It was all just a smokescreen by Ed whose affability really hid another snake. He did remind me a bit of Geoff Travis who was and still is my good friend and brethren." She continues, "He was as honest as the day was long so maybe I extended that trust I gave Geoff to him because he too was bookish, pretty reserved. Not a rock-and-roll guy. Not much small talk. Seemingly very serious and business minded. But unlike Travis, and beneath that almost academic exterior, lurked a fucking poisonous pond scum snake."[26]

Thankfully, as we head into the mid-1980s, we're engulfed in a sea change as music begins to bridge the socioeconomic and racial gulf marked by the meteoric rise of hip hop, reinstating the Bronx as something far removed from the arson attacks and instead as a cradle of creativity and innovation; something ESG channeled in their own musical making efforts. But for such an influential and widely loved LP, *Come Away with ESG* did very little for its creators, not remotely helped by 99 Records imminent demise. The same year that the Scroggins sisters released their debut, another 99 Records artist was facing huge success, but with a bittersweet backlash. In the summer of 1983, their early openers Liquid Liquid released their third EP *Optimo*, produced by Bahlman himself. Bahlman considered "Cavern" the record's most important track and pressed an acetate disc of it and immediately found an avid listenership among club DJs. On the strength of that single, *Optimo* went on to sell upwards of 30,000 copies, a remarkable amount by indie label standards today.

The record's runaway hit was a bit too irresistible though. In October that year, mere months after the EP's release, Sugar Hill Records released Grandmaster and Melle Mel's "White Lines (Don't Do It)," a hip-hop era-defining single that leaned heavily on the group's iconic bassline of "Cavern." Not just that, but you'll hear the telltale conga drum flourishes and even the tracks lyrics as vocalist Sal Principato's opening line of "slip in and out of phenomena" has been mangled and melded into the now-signature hip hop catchphrase "something like a phenomena" (as also referenced in De La Soul's "Ego Trippin' (Part 2)" and LL Cool J's "Phenomenon").

Bahlman made a claim to sue Sugar Hill Records, but despite a successful outcome, legal fees outpaced 99 Records' ability to remain profitable. Bahlman's labor of love had become altogether unbearable. In late 1985, Bahlman decided that he'd finally had enough. In early 1986, the Macdougall

Street premises held a clearance sale before closing its doors forever. Bahlman dropped out of sight and has kept a low profile ever since. Bahlman's breakdown certainly had an impact on the young Scroggins sisters. However, at the same time his vision of 99 Records was being torn down, internal disputes were also happening within ESG. Deborah Scroggins eventually left the group in 1987.

For his investigative look into the label on *The Vinyl Factory*, Tim Ross managed to get some time with Ed's brother, Bill Bahlman, who reflected on his siblings' impressive success for such a short-lived project and its undeniable impact on modern-day music as we know it: "I thought Ed did amazing stuff back then. He worked with artists that otherwise would not have been recorded if he hadn't started his own record label and went about encouraging Glenn Branca and Liquid Liquid and ESG and others into the studio. They may never have put a record out. That legacy still lives on."[27]

As did ESG's, even if the latter half of the 1980s saw the group taking a back seat from music. New families and day-job duties meant that the remainder of the group didn't revisit a recording studio again until the self-released 1987 12" *Bam-Bam Jam*. But the Scroggins sisters' sound was still proliferating the streets of the Bronx, just not necessarily in the way the band would've liked.

3

Sample Credits Don't Pay Our Bills

Liquid Liquid wasn't the only band to fall victim to sampling issues on the 99 label. In the years that followed, both 99 Records and Factory Records encountered severe legal and financial problems. Bahlman spent much of the early 1980s tied up in that infamous legal battle with Sugar Hill Records over the unauthorized sampling of Liquid Liquid's "Cavern" on their (now legendary) hit "White Lines (Don't Do It)." Despite prevailing over the lawsuit, Sugar Hill fell into receivership, and Bahlman was unable to collect his settlement, and he swiftly shut down the label.

Factory Records, too, faced financial trouble before its eventual close a few decades later. By this point, The Haçienda had begun swallowing money, and Tony Wilson was knocking up too many outgoings with his latest signing Happy Mondays famously decamping to glamorous Barbados to lay down a fourth studio release *Yes Please!* (and a handsome 15k budget in tow). With their careers so closely tied to these two entities, ESG suffered the consequences.

One differentiating factor between Wilson and Bahlman's lead was that the former allowed his artists to take their back catalogues with them, many redistributing to alternative indies in the future. It's this sense of business acumen, in hindsight, Renee Scroggins wishes that she and her sisters had possessed when the band was releasing on 99: "I would tell my younger self to be more educated in the music business, business law, and learn more about publishing copyright and the importance of owning your masters," she says. "We love to be artists, but we have to function in a business, and that's the way we run things now."[1] Four decades from the band's debut release, today, all of its operations are run in-house through Renee and her family, from the recording of her music to the distribution and publishing.

It's a lesson no one could have predicted but an element of innocence fellow 99 Records artist Vivien Goldman also saw from afar, as she explains: "Those girls, they were like babes in the woods. They knew nothing. They had no lawyer in the family. They had no role models. They were the absolute essence of punk DIY making it up as they went along."[2] The demise of such an influential label as 99 Records in the New York music scene sits at odds with what else was going on in the same borough that the Scroggins sisters grew up in. And so it was that as one scene was folding into bankruptcy, another culture movement was soaring into stratospheric chart success.

Historically, the Bronx has been positioned as a magnet for creative innovation with its hip hop origin stories. In the recreation room of an apartment building on Sedgwick Avenue right by Bronx Community College on a balmy August evening in 1983 Cindy Campbell was hosting a birthday bash. But the party wouldn't just mark the celebration of Cindy Campbell's birth but also the inception of a new type of music making altogether. Cindy's brother, Clive Campbell, better known to history as DJ Kool Herc and founding father of hip hop, had been refining his break-beat style for a better part of a year. His sister's celebrations, however, put him in front of his biggest crowd to date and one enormous sound system. The success of such an event would begin a grassroots musical revolution.

Born and raised until he was ten years old in Kingston, Jamaica, DJ Kool Herc began spinning records at parties, and between sets his father's band played while he was a teenager in the Bronx. So while many will have you believe that hip hop is an African American musical form, the foundations are actually rooted in the Black Caribbean, with Herc often emulating the style of Jamaican "selectors" as Elena Martinez of the Bronx Music Heritage Centre posits: "Kool Herc was one of the pioneer DJs [of the movement]. Afrika Bambaataa and Grandmaster Flash both had Barbadian roots. Look at Kool DJ Red Alert who's an early DJ. His family's from Antigua and they [came] from the Bronx."[3]

Her partner and artistic director of the Bronx Heritage Music Center, Bobby Sanabria, recalls seeing Kool Herc perform for the first time in a fairly low-key setting considering his subsequent impact on such a cultural movement: "He set up turntables in front of my projects because he went to the Bronx vocational high school right across from where I lived. He was trying to get a big massive sound like you would have in a nightclub."[4] Back then you had to exhibit a certain kind of resourcefulness as a creative person if you wanted anything to bloom in the borough that was sadly still in disarray.

For some, this ingenuity wasn't exactly above the law. On the main strips in the Bronx, young people were throwing bricks through the windows of electronic shops to pilfer the expensive equipment as they continued to try and channel their creativity in ways that they hadn't been able to before. Where everything changed was once it started to get cold. After the summer's evening spent at the co-run Campbell event, the weather began to turn, and schools were beginning to open their doors again. The academics tried to tap into this entrepreneurialism with their students. DIY flyers began making the rounds for upcoming guerilla performances.

While this might sound like the foundations of a surging movement, the voices and DJs behind the hip hop sound were, at this point, still absent from any support on the national airwaves. Author of *God Save The Queens, The Essential History of Women In Hip Hop*, Kathy Iandoli, reflects on the parallels between hip hop's underdog rising and another burgeoning bunch of music makers: "[It's] very similar to what was happening with punk music at the time because mainstream radio was rejecting the concept of what that music was,"[5] she explains. Both genres were frowned upon by the elite. Both genres were scrappy and tenacious, determined to express themselves and their politics through music during times of extreme adversity. And just like its punk peers, hip hop came on the heels of disco dying and artists hunting out the next sound, a title the Bronx specifically was keen to latch hold of for obvious reasons.

"When you're talking about the Bronx, it wasn't regarded as the creative hub that it should have been," believes Iandoli. "The punk scene had downtown Manhattan, and when you're talking about jazz or blues, you think of Harlem, you think of Uptown. The Bronx being able to claim hip hop was very significant because there was nothing there at the time that they were claiming as their own."[6]

This newfound energy of the hip hop scene was a beacon of hope for the burning borough. Schools were going bankrupt. There was no money for music classes, but young people still craved to create or listen to music. Suddenly, there was an influx of adept and technologically savvy sound artists taking their lessons from fellow godfathers of the movement. Grandmaster Flash, the man who gave us the turntable, looked to Grand Wizard Theodore who is heralded for inventing the scratching technique. So against a backdrop of cut funding and limited access to creative resources, this new generation of beatmakers turned to mixing and vinyl crates. But with the borough in flames and many of its cultural establishments closing down, where do they go to listen to music? Martinez picks up.

"They go to parks. They go to schoolyards. They open up the electric lamp pole and plug in there," she recalls, animatedly. "I always say you couldn't do that today. But back then, in the 1970s, when there were burnt buildings all around, shells of buildings, no one cared. They were literally shaped by this devastation to create the music and that sound."[7] Sanabria agrees and notes the significance of their mixing style against more modern-day references. "Early hip hop artists were much more creative than what's happening now because they used to sample records. They used to sample horn lines. They used to sample string arrangements from Broadway shows,"[8] he explains.

Martinez continues that thought: "I remember talking to DJs, the real crate diggers. They were looking at an Israeli folk dance album to get a cool drum. They're not just using pop music, they would find the most off-the-wall stuff to use." It was this flair for digging out killer drum breaks and building onto original material that produced one of the core foundations of hip hop—music sampling. Sampling bridged the class divides often presented with learning musical instruments at a young age. A budding beatmaker need only get their hands on some old records and their parents' sound system and begin embellishing their favorite tracks with limited musical theory.

But for all its ingenuity, sampling also presents an ethical question. Sampling your favorite artists without permission can infringe copyright, yet, at the same time, the process of approval (known as clearance) can be complex and costly. For many fledgling DJs, they're simply priced out or forced to use their poetic license. This might involve them rerecording elements of the track as a nod to the original and, therefore, no longer requiring clearance from the artist (see Liquid Liquid vs. Sugar Hill—the latter would argue the track wasn't technically a sample but a copy by their house band and backup singers).

While their approach might throw up the question of morality, The Sugarhill Gang's influence on the genre and the rise of sampling is undisputed. The band's breakout hit "Rapper's Delight" is often referred to as the first crossover commercial track lending from Chic's second number-one single, "Good Times." As disco was dying, Chic was a victim of the genre's backlash, and the group never had another

No. 1 hit after "Good Times." Instead, guitarist Nile Rodgers and bandleader and late bassist Bernard Edwards took on more producer-based roles to propel the careers of Diana Ross, Sister Sledge, Grace Jones, and, more recently, Pharell Williams: "The next day I bought a copy of 'Rapper's Delight,' but when I looked at the record, Bernard and I weren't even credited. So we filed suit."[9]

Much like Nile Rodgers and bandmate Bernard Edwards, Howard Kaylan and Mark Volman of 1960s rock troupe The Turtles sued American hip hop trio De La Soul for a whopping $2.5 million in 1991. Volman said that "sampling is just a longer term for theft" and that "anybody who can honestly say sampling is some sort of creativity has never done anything creative."[10] Other iconic artists like James Brown, Fab Five Freddy, and Led Zeppelin are among the most readily sampled artists. But it's actually 1960s funk and soul troupe The Winstons' who carry the title of the most sampled artist of all time. Their legendary "Amen Break," a brief drum solo performed by Gregory Sylvester G.C Coleman in 1969 during their track "Amen Brother," has since become the basis for over 5,000 sampled drum loops across hip hop, jungle, breakcore, and drum and bass.

Despite being one of the most sampled recordings in history though, The Winstons received no royalties from its use; bandleader Richard Lewis Spencer said it was unlikely Coleman, who died homeless and destitute in 2006, realized the impact he had made on modern music. It's this same scenario that the Scroggins sisters found themselves in during the early 1980s. Their numbers might not be in the thousands, but their early release "UFO" and its eerie guitar drone has appeared in nearly 550 tracks; that's over 100 more mentions than James Brown's "Funky President" drum fill. And just like the single's namesake, ESG's credit on these songs often remains unidentifiable.

Speaking to Greg Kot of the *Chicago Tribune* ahead of a rare show at the Windy City's Promontory to celebrate ESG's fortieth anniversary, Renee Scroggins reflected on how she felt hearing her riff in other songs and why this often felt like a personal affront: "I would go to different clubs and hear 'UFO' in the background on different records and think someone was stealing from me. Coming from the Bronx in the 1970s where you had all the drugs and gangs, you took that as a personal insult—somebody is stealing my stuff." Ever the professional though, Scroggins reasoned, it was often a fruitless battle to fight, "You deal with it as best you can, but you can't let it get you down, because otherwise, you'd never make music again."[11]

So what makes a fairly unknown, Bronx-based band like ESG so rife for sampling? And, if everyone from gangsta rap stalwarts NWA to, more recently, Rudimental and Emile Sande have sampled their sounds, why do the Scroggins sisters remain nothing more than a footnote in music history? Kathy Iandoli believes that the band's signature fusion of sounds had an impact, along with their predisposition toward recordings with few vocal lines: "When you listen to a track like 'UFO,' you hear multiple genres in one track which makes it so ripe for picking for sampling. It's incredibly difficult when a group is defined by their instrumentals."[12]

Much like The Winstons' drum fill, Renee Scroggins's piercing guitar tone quickly became disconnected from its eerie instrumental setting. Instead, the sample became a stem for others to manipulate into their own music. As soon as that riff was pulled from the Scroggins' stratosphere, the attribution also became lost in the ether: "With ESG, the only ownership was always transferred to the person who took it and that's where there was this big disconnect with the group. It's always become this tagline where the ownership returns back to the white guy," Iandoli muses.

The author references composer David Axelrod as another interesting example of a recording artist whose career was notoriously impacted by his appearances in hip hop records, with everyone from De La Soul to, most notably, Dr. Dre. In fact, during a live performance at the Royal Festival Hall in the early aughts, the seventy-year-old producer observed that he had paid for the night's twenty-six–piece orchestra with the royalties from Dr. Dre's "The Next Episode," which sampled the jerky keyboard motif from his 1967 track "The Edge." "I'm such a hypocrite," he rasped. "I hate sampling because it takes away jobs from musicians, but it allows me to have fun. It's screw-you money." And that's the stark difference between Axelrod versus ESG.

For him, this new generation of music makers brought about his return. It was this rich string of sampling that made the composer fashionable and solvent again. For ESG, the lack of any sample credits—or indeed compensation— only positioned them further into white-label anonymity. To make matters worse, a lot of those big hip hop names leaning on the group's extraterrestrial riff writing were their Bronx-based peers, as Iandoli confirms: "The difference was,

[ESG] were active in the scene. As fast as they were making something, someone was taking it."[13]

She's not wrong. The first known sample of the band's "UFO" appeared in 1982, a full year before their debut record was even released. DJ Dr. Rock and Force MCs perform live at Spring Valley in New York City and there, in and among the jeers as the group enter on stage and begin to rouse the crowd, is the weakened pace of ESG's unrelenting guitar line. Later that decade, notable appearances also crop up on legendary old school hip hop rapper Cutmaster DC's "Brooklyn Is Best" and Public Enemy's "Night of The Living Baseheads"; the former kicks in with the riff after a drum-heavy intro, while the latter uses the somber sound to splice in and out of their final flow.

For the Scroggins sisters, the usage felt raw and unsanctimonious. For the producers, the right to sampling exists at the very essence of the hip hop genre. DJ Premier puts it better in his verse for Gang Stars' "Royalty" as he accuses other artists of reissuing their original records with updated credits detailing where the track has since appeared, insisting that it goes against what hip hop is all about. Judging by the title of ESG's tongue-in-cheek follow-up EP to *Come Away with ESG* in 1992, *Sample Credits Don't Pay Our Bills*, Renee Scroggins also felt fairly violated by the decision to lift from her track.

Such a contentious subject does call for some legal frameworks, but, perhaps, unsurprisingly, given their experiences so far with the music industry's bureaucracy, the legalities weren't in the Scroggins sisters' favor. As a rule of thumb, samples shouldn't exceed thirty seconds or 10 percent of the length of the original song, which, in the case of ESG, suits that guitar riff to a tee. The right to sampling then becomes a two-pronged approach: You can be applauded as an original visionary who dusted off this record in a second-hand record shop to sample the sound, which, once nestled in among your composition, becomes yours and only yours. Or you can attempt to shout out the original, only for the fallout to end up as a battle of the best barristers, which, in the case of a label like 99, didn't bode well either. As Iandoli quips, "There's a reason these things get white labelled where you want all of these credits covered up, right?"[14]

The art of sampling manifests itself differently for all those involved; as a fan, you're fascinated by the whole song. In the case of some of the early aughts samples for ESG (see Nine Inch Nails' "Metal" released in 2000), the riff becomes a subtle bedrock absorbed by the industrial glitches and modular synths. Whereas the producer listens with the concept of "What can I pull from this?" The elements of the original become mere stems to sample and chomp soundbites from: "There's a very 'what you kill, you eat' mentality,"[15] agrees Iandoli.

This is one of the key issues with sampling: permission. The clearance of a track can have devastating ramifications for an artist, as seen with 99 Records' lawsuit against The Sugarhill Gang. In Dr. Dre's continued adventures with accreditations, his record label Aftermath Entertainment faced a similar injunction when its R&B sensation Truth Hurts' chart-topping hit, "Addictive," was sued for not clearing the rights to sampled track "Thoda Resham Lagta Hai" by Indian singer Lata Mangeshkar. Aftermath neglected to clear the rights to sample and, along with Universal Music Group, was slammed with a $500 million lawsuit and injunction preventing further performances or broadcasts of "Addictive."

In the case of ESG, however, by the late 1980s/early 1990s, there was no record label for them to lean on for support when it came to demanding sample credits. Bahlman had retreated from the music industry into academia, and the sisters didn't even bear the rights to their own original recordings. What makes the sampling even more contentious, in this case, is the proximity and the time frames. There's a disconnect with The Nightingale of India, which could be construed as an ode toward another vibrant culture, bringing Mangeshkar's melodies to Western stereos in a scene she wouldn't ordinarily find herself in. Conversely, the Scroggins sisters were still touring the New York circuit with the original song prominent in their setlists. Iandoli agrees it was the locality that felt particularly painful.

> With ESG, they were robbing their neighbour. They were robbing their peers. It's definitely not right to rob Lata Mangeshkar or rob anybody, but in the interest of maintaining the integrity of an art form that originated as a response to being robbed, from the idea of stealing from your next-door neighbour made that a more offensive crime in music because those girls deserved a shot just as much as anyone else.[16]

Maintaining the integrity of the art form is another area that many sampled artists have fallen prey to. Take Enya's iconic "Boadicea," which appears on Fugees' "Ready or Not." In a

Forbes interview in 2016, the Irish songwriter reflected on the importance of a shared sentiment that takes from your own musical archive: "We had to feel a link between what the song was about and the original song that we had written." She continues, "If an artist is going to sample a piece of music, then you get to hear it, that's what's important to me. There are a lot of songs that I've been happy to sample because it is introducing the music to another generation but I just feel it's right to approach the artist."[17]

Back in the Bronx, Renee Scroggins explained her antagonism toward unlicensed samplers in an early aughts article for *The Independent*: "To the people who clear it with us—thank you! To the people who don't, you're a pain in the a** and I'm gonna come after you! You're taking food out of my kids' mouths," she shared, pointedly. "Sometimes, also, I don't like the way they use it. Really negative, woman-beating type of songs. I've been in situations with domestic violence, so I don't appreciate any song glorifying domestic violence using my music. Go get your own damn music!"[18]

And this is the second fundamental issue when it comes to sampling: What is the context and message of the track, and does that align with your own artistic views? In that same case of Enya vs Fugees, it's been reported that the musician switched up her stance after confirming the band were not "gangsta rappers." Her manager, Nicky Ryan, spoke of the incident in the *Irish Voice* in 1997, "From a management point of view, we had our own worries. Was this band of the pro-crime/drugs/gangsta variety so prevalent at the time in the States and would Enya's fans react to hearing her music on such an album?"[19]

After some rudimentary discussions with her daughter Ebony who confirmed that the Fugees were anticrime and drugs, instead with their own positive messaging, Ryan was keen to find an amicable solution to address the permission breach. In the end, Enya resolved her issues with the Fugees after Sony Records agreed to put a sticker on all copies of *The Score* crediting her for the sample. Sadly for ESG, "UFO" has been predominantly used in hip hop tracks that aren't necessarily dripping with gender parity when it comes to lyricism or indeed their music videos. A characteristic of the genre that hadn't passed Renee Scroggins by when she reflected on the situation during an interview together in 2015.

"There's no way that me, Renee, as a woman, would allow a man to take that song and sing over it about 'you bitch' and 'you whore'. No, no. That's what disturbs me. Sometimes people just use the whole song and rap straight over it and it's very disturbing."[20] In 1993, over a decade on from ESG releasing their early EP, The Notorious B.I.G's debut single "Party & Bullshit" lifted the band's "UFO" riff to form the bedrock of the track alongside warm keys and 4/4 beats. In the first verse, the rapper launches into a diatribe about his early school days cutting classes and squeezing asses. Fast forward to Moet popping and hoe hopping in verse two and you get the feeling that Biggie wasn't exactly a monogamous man.

The same year 2Pac released "Peep Game," on his second studio album *Strictly For My N.I.G.G.A.Z*, which also features ESG's signature guitar line as he interrogates a female counterpart, eventually condemning her as a hoochie looking for some swag. In this case, "hoochie" is a derogatory term used to describe a young woman who has had many casual sexual partners or who dresses or behaves in a sexually provocative way. Scroggins felt a real conflict with this positioning, particularly as the bandleader of the Black sisters: "I'm a woman, there's no way I would support those messages."[21] The sample is particularly bittersweet given the meaning behind "Peep Game," which encourages us to open our eyes and recognize what's going on. For Scroggins, the imbalance was all too apparent. "Sometimes it's brought to my attention, the music is not under my control, another company run by men, but a lot of the time there's nothing that I can do about it."[22]

One of the wooliest areas of sampling is what happens if an artist does go through the proper channels to request a sample but it isn't authorized and their vision rests on that refrain or musical motif. As the old saying goes, imitation is the best form of flattery as we see certain musicians taking matters into their own hands and rewriting another's musical components so they can keep the rights to themselves. Sort of like Taylor's version, only for any track produced in modern music to date. This was the case with the Sugarhill Gang's infamous "White Lines," which doesn't actually contain a sample of Liquid Liquid's "Cavern" but an extensively mimicked version using their house band and backup singers.

This issue was brought to light again in a more recent case back in 2013, when Portishead's Geoff Barrow accused the Weeknd of sampling Portishead's "Machine Gun" in his track "Belong to the World" without permission. Taking to Twitter, Barrow said that the Weeknd claimed that his song didn't use a sample "or enough likeness to 'Machine Gun' to warrant any infringement ... or credit." But the following year, the Portishead founder opened up the debate again by sharing a photo of a letter from early 2013, showing the Weeknd's management requesting clearance to sample "Machine Gun" for what was then titled "You Belong to the World." Does this suggest that the Weeknd took a different approach after being refused the sample and instead turned his hand to a similar beat?

Portishead are undisputed when it comes to their impact on music, practically inventing the Bristol-based trip-hop movement. Without the English electronic band, would there be Tricky, or Sneaker Pimps and Morcheeba for that matter? They are now part of the DNA of British music. Similarly, when it comes to pioneering parties, ESG has been cited as "the coolest band in NYC. No question" by hip hop titans Beastie Boys, but there's no way that Renee Scroggins would air her beef like Barrows. Instead, the band remain unknown in most musical circles despite their single providing a fundamental bedrock to hundreds of chart-topping records across four decades.

For Iandoli, the recognition feels necessary even if the Scroggins clan might've actively taken a step outside of the mainstream media

Maybe Renee doesn't want to be a part of the matrix. But in those circles, she needs to be held up as royalty. The flowers should be given even if she puts them in a vase in her home and just stares at them and doesn't post them on Instagram. You can't be like, "Well, maybe she should have made herself well known."

Was it ESG's responsibility to argue their rights over each individual record like Enya over in her castle in Dublin? Or did a band like the Scroggins sisters demand a team of musical professionals and savvy label types to help straighten these sample credits out from the start? With 99 Records folding before the end of the 1980s, ESG never stood a chance.

"There's a lot of revisionist history. There's a lot of people who are backtracking because nothing was written down anyway [which] makes it almost impossible for ESG to turn around and be like, 'Hey, we were actually the first to pioneer the combination of proto-punk and funk,'" says Iandoli. "All they have is the music to press play and long lists on *whosampled dot net*. It's all they got. It is heartbreaking." As Jessica Meiselman reflected in her 2016 article for *FACT* magazine, "Now for producers, it's not just a case of 'Should I sample this?' but 'Can I get away with it?' "[23] And, in the case of an often overlooked band like ESG, the nameless legacy gives the permission slip for so many to assume they can.

For both Portishead and ESG, their tracks occupy a broad and genre-bending space, which means that a multitude of artists sees their relevance, regardless of their own style or sound. Their songs offer snippets into musical moments, ready-made to be cut and pasted accordingly, particularly for a track like "UFO," which begins with a horrorcore siren screech played out on the guitar. Perfect for when you want a dark moody hip hop song. Then, there's the heavy bass, conjuring up huge house sounds for those tracks that needed a bang. Not to mention that more industrial sound—the tinny demo recording that sounds like it's been created in somebody's garage.

In the case of "UFO," ESG's mutating rhythms become the canvas rather than the product of all the brush strokes from a group of hard working teenagers at home in the Bronx, schooling themselves with instruments to try and stay off the streets. The fact their early EP single provided such a catalyst for other artists to express themselves should be commended. But when that comes without the rightful attribution then, as Iandoli puts it, "it's very difficult for a group like that to get on a stage and play their songs and be like, 'Does this sound familiar?'"[24]

Sadly in the case of ESG, sampling copyright is just one of a multitude of areas in which the Scroggins sisters struggle to gain recognition, hinting at a far wider, more systemic issue with the music industry as a whole. Why else would a band that has had such a pronounced impact on modern dance music as we know it remain a footnote in history? Iandoli is quick to respond, "It's really quite simple. Anything in music that's revolutionized, they don't want to give the credit to a woman." We see it even in the base language we use to polarize our leading figures in pop music by gender.

Our everyday conversations are shaping the way we position our artists, caring more about their genitalia than genius. Longstanding pop icons like Diana Ross and Mariah Carey are constantly being accused of "diva-ish demands," while, despite their similarly lofty status and outrageous rider requests (looking at you and your square watermelons, Axl Rose), their male counterpoints are doused with a bit more humor. Freddie Mercury, the undisputed male diva, fronts a band called Queen; Mick Jagger prances and swaggers.

It seems the traits that are seen as assertive, endearing, or humorous in a man are unacceptable in a woman.

As the saying goes, behind every man is a great woman, and this seems to be the case so often in music. Look at the power struggle between Dolly Parton and Porter Wagoner or the double marginalization Aretha Franklin faced when she emerged from society's fringes into a racially segregated country. Even for a band in the depths of a male-heavy grunge scene like Nirvana, there was a lightning rod-like feminist firecracker Kathleen Hanna behind one of the group's most influential songs. Iandoli agrees: "No one ever talks about how Kathleen Hanna is the reason why we have Kurt Cobain, really? Even the joke of Kurt Smells Like Teen Spirit is the framework for Nirvana's popularity. Whenever there's a woman behind the creation, it's 'how can we take this away from her?'"

To this day, ESG remains without their crucial credit to a decade-spanning influence and artistry. Never ones to bemoan their situation though, and as their 2006 record confirmed, the Scroggins sisters kept on moving.

4

Keep on Moving

There would be an almost ten-year gap between ESG's debut, *Come Away with ESG*, and their next body of recorded work, the spiritedly titled *Sample Credits Don't Pay Our Bills* in 1992. During that time, they tapped back into the mission at the heart of the band, taking their unstoppable beats on the road performing the songs that had since begun proliferating DJs' crates from Manhattan to Manchester. This commitment to touring has become a staple for the group as they've continued to appear on stages across the globe for their fans well into Renee Scroggins's sixties.

Throughout their decade-spanning career, the Bronx-born band has performed everywhere from the intimate Park Stage of Glastonbury to the closing night of Larry Levan's iconic New York discotheque in 1987. The prototype for the modern dance club, Paradise Garage, or "Gay-rage" as was often quipped with its devoted crowds largely made up of sexual and ethnic minorities, is said to have been a direct inspiration for London's own Ministry of Sound. A Scroggins send-off feels like a fitting ode to such an archetypal institution as the band is often coined as the first proto hip hop girl gang and has long been embraced within the queer community. As Renee explained to the *San Francisco Examiner* ahead of their Hard Pride show in 2015, "In New York, the LGBT community has always supported us so I find it a great pleasure that I'm able to give a little bit back."[1]

On that infamous night, the sisters shared the bill with Gwen Guthrie (famed for her time as a backup singer to Aretha Franklin and landmark hit "Ain't Nuthin' Goin' On But the Rent") and Queen of House Liz Torres. They were also notoriously the only outfit allowed to perform live, a prospect that was becoming increasingly rare for shows in the city as the remaining clubs claimed that it was too expensive to set up for performances, with most recording artists releasing lip-synced TV versions of their material. Asking the frontwoman and founder to reflect on the last hurrah of the King Street kingpin, Renee Scroggins recalls the impressive tech setup (lightyears away from those scaffolding-supported days of The Haçienda): "Paradise Garage to this day has the best sound system I have ever heard. I've played in clubs all over the world but nothing comes close to theirs."

But it was the incredible reception the venue received that Renee recalls vividly, and, despite an air of sorrow, the band and building stayed true to their signature spirit by keeping the groove going until the bitter end: "It was packed. I remember feeling like a sardine in the can, we could hardly get up to the stage!" she recalls, with a hearty chuckle. "They couldn't get people in, they were turning people away. It was a nonstop party for two days. We played the first night and then we came back and played the last night. I loved the sound but there was some sadness thinking that this place was no longer going to be there."[2]

Paradise Garage's farewell party wouldn't be the only seismic popular culture moment for ESG that decade though as the band's penchant for a dance rhythm and pop hook became synonymous with bustling club appearances. Their early release "Moody" was later picked up by the production company at Magellan Films who asked the band to perform in Nicolas Cage's 1988 movie, *Vampire's Kiss*: The group appears decked out in crisp black and white tie with monogrammed congas on the stage of a jam-packed bar, as Cage sidles up to his love interest over cocktails and candlelight. All of the individual members of the group still appear on the cast list as "Band Member," except for bassist at the time Leroy Glover, who failed to sign a release form on the day of the shoot.

When asked about the silver screen performance for Culture Collide, Renee Scroggins reflected on the differences between the band's efficiency in the studio compared to a multimillion cine setup and how the cameo continues to credit their efforts, unlike their chart-topping peers: "You know what was interesting about that? That scene was like a minute long. Did you know it took us twelve hours to shoot that? We actually got into the union because of that, The Screen Actors Guild, so that was cool. And I still get residuals from that to this day."[3]

But even with their Screen Actors Guild status, by the end of the 1980s, major crossover fame and earnings had escaped ESG despite a string of subsequent releases. Their first fifteen years on the road were curated and compiled into *ESG Live!* and released in 1995 on Nega Fulô Records. That same year, Renee added her daughter, Nicole, and niece, Chistelle, to ESG as the group began to evolve. While compilations (2000's *A South Bronx Story*) and reissues have continued to keep the Scroggins' sound alive, it was their era-defining debut *Come Away with ESG* decades after its release that ushered in a resurgence for the band, proving that its innovative rhythms and songwriting continued to influence into a new millennium.

The end of the century also marked the dissolution of another band who were intrinsic in carving space for women in the world during the early 1990s riot grrrl movement. Two years after releasing their second studio album, *Reject All American*, in 1995, riot grrrl ringleader Kathleen Hanna and her Bikini Kill bandmates amicably disbanded. After the group's breakup, Hanna turned inwards toward bedroom beatmaking producing a self-titled album released under the pseudonym The Julie Ruin. In an attempt to bring the project out of her home studio and onto the stage, Hanna enlisted the skills of friend and zine editor Johanna Fateman. But when the songwriter relocated to New York City to attend art school, Hanna followed her lead and the pair (alongside filmmaker Sara Benning) launched an entirely different act in the early aughts.

Leaving behind the fury and freneticism of Bikini Kill, electroclash outfit Le Tigre channeled the same half-hour dancefloor affirmations the Scroggins sisters had been championing some twenty years prior, a reference that Hanna admits readily: "Bikini Kill really loved bands like the Slits and the Raincoats and ESG. [Their] *Come Away with ESG* really influenced Le Tigre."[4] The Bronx-based band's impact can certainly be heard in the group's debut self-titled record, which landed sixteen years on from ESG's own inaugural efforts. But despite being nearly two decades its senior, *Come Away with ESG's* tinny lo-fi beats and simple fuzzed out chord progressions are there in Le Tigre's feminist jibe on filmmaker John Cassavetes, "What's Yr Take on Cassavetes." Likewise, the dominant bassline and rudimentary riffs of "Eau D'bedroom Dancing" reek of early 80s production values, not to mention that song title which feels like a missed opportunity for a Scroggins sisters' signature scent.

Hanna wasn't the only stalwart in the New York music scene reveling once more in ESG's discography for inspiration. Critics were touting a whole new wave of raucous "dance punk" that plagued indie discos at the turn of the millennium. In Elizabeth Goodman's *Meet Me in the Bathroom*, James Murphy and Juan Maclean both recount arriving in New York City expecting to be immersed in the vibrant music scene that birthed agit-punks Liquid Liquid and instead found a lot of House music and some tired indie rock bands. Propelled by this stagnant setting, Maclean formed Six Finger Satellite, one of the first bands in the 1990s to revisit those angular guitars once more, with none other than a certain James Murphy manning their sound.

Murphy, who many would argue engineered this revival in the noughties, himself admits to hunting out ESG's LPs among their 99 Records peers and Cologne krautrockers Can in the vinyl crates: "When I was DJing, I became kind of cool for a moment, which was a total anomaly," he explains to journalist John Doran. Murphy goes on to explain how his record picks would go on to position him as the "cool rock disco guy," and in a state of fear around losing this new found acceptance in hip circles, he penned the band's 2002 single

"Losing My Edge." The same track inadvertently taps into some of the feelings omnipresent for the Scroggins sisters during their career as Murphy expands, "Then it became a wider thing about people who grip onto other people's creations like they are their own."[5]

Yet while the dance-punk scene of New York in the noughties felt like an incestuous tag team of creative collaborations and cameos—Al Doyle of LCD Soundsystem also performed in synth nerds Hot Chip while his frontman Murphy engineered The Rapture's *Echoes* and later the dance-heavy return for Arcade Fire in *Reflektor*—ESG's dance-punk pedigree was in a league of its own in early 1980s New York. As their early releases and studio time with Martin Hannett prove, their songwriting was more akin to what was happening in Manchester. Digitizing the layered rhythms we find in ESG's debut, the in-house producer at Factory Records introduced Joy Division to the Synare, a synthesizer controlled through a percussive pad rather than a keyboard, which launched in the mid-1970s and was also favored by fellow postpunks The Cure. Just like the Scroggins sisters bringing "The Beat" on *Come Away with ESG*, the synare dished out a motoric rhythm, providing a backbone to many of our late-night indie clubs across the country.

Propelled by these new-era champions and a fresh desire for propulsive beats, the Bronx-based sister troupe began popping up on international festival lineups in the midst of this dance-punk odyssey. Not content to just ride the revival wave on their existing back catalogue, though, ESG returned with their first new material in over a decade: 2002's *Step Off* via Soul Jazz Records. The returning record secured them a slot at annual British music festival All Tomorrow's Parties in 2004, amusingly alongside their new-era dance-punk protégées and longtime fans Le Tigre and LCD Soundsystem. A few years later, and with another new record in tow (2006's *Keep on Moving*), the band performed under the steel lighting rigs and branded backdrops of Barcelona's long-running Primavera Festival.

Yet while Europe, and particularly the UK, has embraced the Scroggins sisters as their own over the years, the Bronx remains at the heart of ESG's story. And just as the borough has been heralded as the birthplace of hip hop, New York—in a wider guise—continues to prove that it's capable of churning out seismic movements that have gone on to shape America's identity as the early aughts proved. Returning to Goodman's *Meet Me in the Bathroom*, the author calls the time period "the last true rock'n'roll music scene" of New York and shares how the sound of Manhattan went mainstream at the start of a new millennium.

Goodman details the rise of this rebellion against the rap-rock proliferating the charts at the time, with a dizzyingly large cast of key players, including fellow New York siren Karen O[rzolek] who agrees the movement was palpable: "There was a faint stirring of the music scene," she explains. "[But] it would positively explode in two years' time. It felt like the people who would catalyse that explosion were only just finding each other, hanging out, discovering music they like that would kick it all into gear."[6]

For Orzolek, ESG was an instrumental discovery for her as a songwriter when she picked up their 2000 compilation album in her local record shop, as she recalls. "When I found

A South Bronx Story at Kim's Video and Music on St Marks in the East Village, it knocked my socks off. First off, it sounded like a Bruce Davidson photo. The ones he took of the New York subways in the 1980s; so much grit, so much heat yet stone cold, so much freakin' attitude."

So formative was the record that, a year later, after an unsuccessful stint performing as acoustic duo Unitard, Orzolek and guitarist Nick Zinner threw themselves into the already burgeoning art punk scene in the form of righteous racketeers Yeah Yeah Yeahs. The band's debut self-titled EP, which came out under their own label in 2001, in particular, channels the similarly stripped-back verses of an ESG arrangement, which Orzolek admits wasn't entirely unintentional: "When Nick and I started writing songs for Yeah Yeah Yeahs, it was like 'I want to be like ESG.' Even though we cannot touch their level of New York cool, we ought to learn from the masters."

But for Orzolek, it was more than just the dance beats and Renee's tough love lyricism teeming with sexuality; these sisters were subverting the archetype of what it meant to be punk and provided a readymade catalyst of representation for other young women to follow, particularly those with more diverse backgrounds: "This music by these sisters, I hadn't heard women throw down like that. Most of my influences up to that point were bands with charismatic white boys at the helm. Hearing ESG struck a whole different chord with me. It was ladies I could emulate. The most badass ladies on the planet as far as I was concerned."

While many teenagers in the early aughts saw Orzolek as a figurehead of power and possibility, the decade's signature rock star's tenacity and beer-spewing spectacle was stoked by the slow-burning embers of a band like ESG. As Goodman expertly puts it in *Meet Me in the Bathroom*, "I found that everyone was in awe of her and still is. The era produced some great rock stars—Julian Casablancas, Jack White, and James Murphy—but almost all of them name-checked Karen as the barometer for the era's essential feel, this blend of youth and abandon."

That same youthful abandon was rising out of the ashes of the Bronx in the late 1970s, an earlier period where people felt friction between what was being pushed by the media. The city of New York was in conflict; the sheen of the disco balls of Manhattan no longer represented the grit and gumption of the working-class boroughs where people lived. A similar discord could be heard sounding out at the end of the century, as Orzolek recalls: "Rock, or whatever you call it, was in a terrible state. It needed a demolition job. Many of my fellow bands wanted to take the scraps and junk from the junkyard."[7] Likewise, in the early 1980s, chart-toppers like Blondie gleaned from the catchy pop thrills of disco, skyrocketing them to fame. While the Scroggins sisters took a more DIY approach, forging together their sounds from the snatches of percussion heard in St. Mary's Park—something raw and without pretension—pulling their discography together all before they were even able to legally enter a bar.

Orzolek was inspired by this streamlined approach, seeking out the essential sounds to make a track sing without new wave's more processed performance with synthesizers, sequencers, and technological rigidity: "We were stripping it down to what's most raw, [to] get the most bang for your buck with the least amount of instruments"[8]—the exact same essence of songwriting the Scroggins sisters had channeled two decades earlier with their meager instruments and fledgling songwriting skills. By tapping into that youthful abandon, *Come Away with ESG* ... sets a band like ESG apart from their lip-synching, TV-ready New York peers. These sisters were on a leftfield trajectory, taking risks and tapping into the unknown. With the simplicity of youth on their side, the Scroggins sisters ended up producing a full length that sounds like essential New York at a time when the community around them felt disparate and in flux.

And so in the midst of this postpunk resurgence in the early aughts across the state again, the embers of ESG's intrigue were slowly beginning to reignite—an unexpected peak of interest that led to something of a momentous occasion for Orzolek. Twenty-five years after laying down demos with Martin Hannett, ESG returned to Radio Music City Hall in 2009 to support Yeah Yeah Yeahs for an emotional hometown show. The art rockers decked out what is ordinarily the home to American precision dance troupe The Rockettes with confetti cannons and huge inflatable eyeballs for the occasion (arguably way ahead of Muse's own fabled UV balls that would be suspended from Wembley Stadium five years later). When Orzolek and her band took to the stage for their encore, she candidly dedicated the set to their opener ESG ("Where would we be without ESG?") and the band's parents.

"Playing Radio City Music Hall was a career-high for us. I remember [ESG] sounding great and being so grateful to have them there with us,"[9] Orzolek says, although she does have one regret from the proceedings:

The absurdity was that we were too shy and awkward to go over and say hello and meet them. Intimidated, I guess. I was kicking myself for years and years after that. I finally wrote them an email a couple of years ago telling them how much it meant to us that they played and apologizing for not having the guts to say hello. They wrote back a nice acknowledgement though maybe they were really like, "Wait, who are you and when did we play with you?" Serves us right.

Three years on from performing at Radio Music City Hall with Yeah Yeah Yeahs, ESG released *Closure* and announced their last tour with a final West Coast appearance performing at San Francisco's Pride Party in 2012. The event was so momentous that the night saw the band's original lineup come together with siblings Renee, Marie, and Valerie all performing at the San Francisco show, a feat that hadn't happened for several years at this point. The night felt particularly important to demonstrate ESG's long-standing support of the queer community too, as Renee explained, gratefully: "I'm happy to support the LGBT community because they are great supporters of ESG, and we love our fans. All of our fans!"[10]

Yet even with their intentions to bring the party to an end, the Scroggins sisters were lured back onto the stage for a very special UK show a few years later. Turns out heavy rock juggernauts Metallica weren't the only 1980s icons making their debut appearance at Glastonbury in 2014, as ESG performed an intimate set at the festival's iconic Park Stage the same year. In a similarly lofty setting, the group were also revealed on the lineup for James Lavelle's Meltdown Festival at London's Thames-facing arts venue, the Southbank Centre, alongside the Unkle cofounders other choice picks with disco selector DJ Harvey and Orange Juice's Edwyn Collins. Finally, it seemed that the Bronx-born troupe was sidling up against their fellow pioneering peers in the music world.

Buoyed by the gravity of these gig bookings and with a tight live show in tow, the band were back in the UK just over a year later for a headline tour on what was (again) pegged as their final European visit. The news of the band's return sparked a particularly profound moment for international voice artist Anne Gallien. While living in London during the late 1990s, Gallien went along to a private show in Kentish Town to see the group, invited along by her partner of the time Grammy-award winning composer Richard David James, better known as Aphex Twin: "When I saw them on the stage, I was quite blown away by those three women. It always stayed with me,"[11] Gallien shares, earnestly.

Inspired by the sisters' minimalist arrangements, Gallien formed her own band, the Veees, in 2011, which quickly caught the attention of aforementioned artistic cornerstone Geoff Barrow of Portishead who offered for the Veees' EP to come out via his own Invada Records. But when Gallien, now living in the West Country, heard that ESG was returning back to the UK for some shows nearly twenty years after seeing them live in the late 1990s, her primal performing instincts kicked in: "I saw that they were coming to Bristol and I said, 'I'm not going to be in the fucking crowd, I have to be on stage with them.'"[12]

Gallien fired off a message to the band's Facebook page sharing her recently released music and the story of how that impromptu Kentish Town show had impacted her over the years as a performing artist: "I never thought that I would get a reply from a personal email!" she admits, clearly astonished. "I had a reply straight away though saying, 'Do you want to be our backing vocalist in a week's time in Bristol, Paris and then in Brighton? We like your music.' I mean, no rehearsal, just singing. I was like 'What the fuck?' "[13]

True to her word, Gallien turned up at the venue in Bristol and was quickly ushered in as backing vocalist alongside frontwoman Renee, daughter Nicole, son Nicholas, and long-standing drummer Leroy Glover: "I did [the tour] all by my own goodwill but it was like a dream come true. The fact that [Renee] liked my music, I was very honoured."[14] During the string of UK live shows in 2015 though, Scroggins was struggling with a latent knee injury after falling out of a tour van in Leeds. Despite the four rods put into it, she was still awaiting surgery that winter. (In keeping with ESG's steadfast determination, at the show in question, Renee admits she simply soaked her knee backstage, popped a couple of painkillers, wrapped it up, and hit the stage.)

Gallien was wise to Renee's condition and the distress the frontwoman faced as she prepared for another night on stage in the back rooms of the latest venue: "She was already in pain and on steroids. I was giving her reiki each night before the gig but it was obvious Renee just wanted to be back in the hotel straightaway. She didn't have the energy at all. We thought she was going to collapse each night, that's how bad it was." Whether it was a side effect of the heavy medication or the immense pain the elder Scroggins was having to self-manage, Gallien recalls her character often appearing quite unyielding, "She was not an easy person to be with. I would call her the iron woman, 'the femme de fer.'"[15]

But after having fought multiple lawsuits since the band's inception thanks to the industry's unrelenting handle of their music through a previously unregulated sample trade, is it surprising that Renee Scroggins might be cautious to let her guard down? Gallien reasons the same: "[She's] had to face a lot of difficult stuff and that's why I have lots of respect for her carrying the band with a new generation. When I was part of ESG, on a deep level, it really felt like a family. Even though she was difficult to deal with, I had this warmth towards her."[16]

Carrying a band into a new generation isn't without its struggles and not just when it comes to licensing and sampling ethics. Now, self-releasing their material, ESG was keen to showcase some of their most recent material to their newfound fans, but, as Gallien recalls, it was the classics that kept up the momentum: "The most popular tracks that we were playing [were tracks like] 'You Make No Sense,' 'You're No Good,' 'Dance,' 'Moody.' … They were the ones that everyone was really dancing to, the old tracks. My impression was that the new stuff was not as popular."[17]

But popularity has never been the cornerstone for a band like ESG who have long flown under the radar because even in the face of apparent anonymity, their long-standing fan base's loyalty cannot be touched. The Scroggins sisters' basic beat formations and simple, playground chants atop those minimal bass lines generate something primal and instinctive within anyone who hears it, making it impossible not to reciprocate: "Brutal but not violent like punk," as Gallien explains. "You can't help but just move. Your body responds to it so there's something a bit tribal about it."[18] With their multigenerational impact into a new century and legion of cult fans—from LCD Soundsystem frontman James Murphy touting their vinyl in his DJ crates to Orzolek coining them "the most badass ladies on the planet"—it's fair to say that ESG has formed an unassuming musical tribe like no other.

5

Forty Years of Dancing: ESG's Decade-Spanning Legacy

Come Away with ESG landed in 1981, the same year that director Daniel Petrie's *Fort Apache, The Bronx* premiered at cinemas. Filmed on location in the Bronx, *Fort Apache* told a truth-based account of a dedicated cop's determination to bring justice to his precinct. But the film also showed the fires, the devastation, and the gang mentality. The local community called the producers out for their misrepresentation of the neighborhood and particularly its portrayal of ethnic minorities at the time. Yet even with such fierce opposition, the film opened at number one at the US box office and only served as a further catalyst to position the Bronx as the burning borough.

That's one of the reasons that ESG's debut record is such an important musical milestone in time. Those eleven tracks are a rebuttal against the assumed violent or fractious output of the area. The Bronx represents a melting pot of influences, from its days as El Condado de la Salsa (the center of salsa) in the 1940s to its rebirth as the cradle of hip hop in the 1990s—as does *Come Away with ESG*. The full length fuses together the broad beats brought together in the borough. There's the rollicking rhythms of the Latino groups playing congas in the park across from the projects. The percussive funk shuffle of previous tenants like Howard King (the drummer of funk and soul group Mtume) whose late-night drum sessions could be felt pulsing through the tower blocks, as Bronx Music Heritage Center co-artistic director Bobby Sanabria explained, "Nobody called the cops. He must have played for 10 minutes straight, full volume and then I remember somebody yelling out from the window. 'Yo, why the fuck did you stop, man?'"

Frontwoman Renee Scroggins's cool drawl delivery sat happily alongside hip hop's first lady Sha Rock in early Funky 4+1 jams (the emcee also grew up in the South Bronx), while ESG's refusal to run with the standard chorus-verse-chorus song structures earned them an admirable place within the underground no wave scene of the early 1980s, a movement that encouraged freedom and inclusivity. Anyone could pick up an instrument and make a sound—a mantra their mother, Helen Scroggins, had shared with her daughters when gifting them instruments one Christmas. With their stripped-back minimalism, wandering grooves, and rapping snares, *Come Away with ESG* even boasts the rudimentary drive of drum and bass, long before the genre was coined out of the UK's jungle scene in the early 1990s.

Just as the Bronx "has always been a great cauldron of stuff going on musically and artistically,"[1] the Scroggins sisters' iconic debut serves up all of its sounds in just over thirty, hip-shaking, minutes. The borough, and the band's South Bronx story, will always be the backdrop to this record and that unbreakable bond creates a certain synergy between the two parties. Martinez agrees, adding that the Bronx boasts "this weird duality. We have the negative but, on the other hand, that also gives us authenticity [and] people want authentic experiences."

That's what you'll find listening to ESG's debut (and their continuing discography across the decades): The original sound of four sisters coming together to create something dynamic and refreshing, recognizing their own cultural heritage and forging those myriad influences into something wholly unique that still, to this day, feels timely and toe-tappingly tempting. Like the siren call of Karen O in the early noughties through a rack of skinny jeans and artfully messy male haircuts, ESG's greatest legacy is how they radiate a sense of truth about themselves and the world around them, inspiring their listeners to do the same.

The enduring influence of ESG's music cannot be overstated. Who else could claim the admiration of their South Bronx neighbors in the nascent hip hop community, Larry Levan at the Paradise Garage, and the postpunk worlds of both the UK and the United States? To chart the Scroggins sisters' influence across the decades begins with their New York City peers in the early 1980s, as hip hop troupe Beastie Boys confirmed in their heavyweight bestseller in 2018: "ESG were the coolest band in NYC in 1983, no question."[2] The same decade, the Scroggins sisters were welcomed into the Factory Records' fold. Their polyrhythms and genre-bending sound were more akin to the Manchester cool of A Certain Ratio or The Haçienda DJ Mike Pickering's

Latin funk dance troupe Quango Quango (the latter teemed their fusion with a Grace Jones pop sing along, but the rhythm sticks and timbales remain).

Heading into the 1990s, the band's impact was so prolific that the references became hard to track and, sadly, attribute. A foundation of the hip hop era, the rise of sampling saw producers reusing or manipulating audio from one recording to another, ranging from entire bars of music to individual drum hits and melodies. Branded as "working-class' Black answer to punk" by David McNamee in *The Guardian* and like no wave's belief that we can all be creators, sampling democratized music as an art form, particularly across race and class with so many cuts to arts funding across the Bronx.

With their predisposition toward recordings with few vocal lines, ESG's catalogue was ripe for reuse. The difference was, as author Kathy Iandoli quipped, "[ESG] were active in the scene. As fast as they were making something, someone was taking it."[3] During the 1990s, everyone from NWA ("Real Niggaz Don't Lie") to Notorious BIG ("Party and Bullshit") gleaned from the group's infamous track "UFO," their eerie guitar line sounding out across hundreds of drum-led rap spats. Even R&B girl group TLC had a crack with "Das Da Way We Like 'Em'" as they sang about understanding the depths of the 1990s woman over Renee Scroggins's signature lead line.

By the time the noughties came around, despite being twenty years out from their debut, there was a resurgence in the band's pioneering sound, not least thanks to the dance-punk revival in the music industry led by mega fan, and fellow New Yorker, James Murphy of LCD Soundsystem. For some groups, ESG's influence was injected into their DNA as the Yeah Yeah Yeahs fed into the vanguard of dual musicians in a bid to keep things stripped back (see also The White Stripes, Death From Above, and, less successfully, The Ting Tings) with frontwoman Karen O at the helm, much like Scroggins herself.

Others were more upfront about the homage, as Aussie-American experimentalists Liars demonstrated, rewriting "UFO" into an eerie aggro reimagining on their 2001 (and ambitiously titled) record *They Threw Us All in a Trench and Stuck a Monument on Top*. "Tumbling Walls Buried Me in the Debris" channeled the same lo-fi execution as ESG; at points vocalist Angus Andrew sounds like he's singing into a beaten-up tin can. For the sisters, this production value was most likely a reflection of the gear at the time. For Liars, it was a nod to the acerbic, angular punk they grew up listening to. But while the Brooklyn-born bunch knowingly referenced the band, a lot of the critics were none the wiser to the obvious ode. Instead, *Pitchfork* called the song "disorientingly repetitive, with a sinking, introverted melody, Zen-like chimes and a beat that sounds like the delusion-sequence music from a P.O.W. film."[4] Like the title track of their most sampled music to date, ESG had some close encounters with fame in cult circles but remain unidentified by the masses.

But then, perhaps, that's been part of the group's appeal all along. "All the good things are undercover," reasons Sil Kelly, drummer of Argentinian postpunks Las Kellies. The pair is just one example of a new guard of rising musicians tapping into the, now, decade-spanning career of the

Scroggins sisters alongside fellow jittering art-punk types Shopping, with their razor-thin bass grooves and terse vocal delivery. Originally performing as a trio, Sil alongside Ceci Kelly (vocals and guitar) were completed by British bass player Betty (real name, Julia Worley), and it was here that the duo was first introduced to ESG—twenty-two years on from *Come Away with ESG*'s initial release—"Betty was from Portsmouth but we were living together here in Argentina. She was showing us a lot of very cool music but when we heard ESG, we felt something different," Ceci explains. "We were amazed because of the simplicity and the ambiance they create with almost nothing. That was our start, our north; make some great things with almost nothing."[5]

This intention runs through the band's latest release, *Suck My Tangerine*, with its minimalistic dual-pronged dynamic between Ceci's spiked guitar strokes and Sil's taut beats. They're similarly sparing when it comes to lyrics, not just instrumentation, often centering on a repeat or a refrain, like the ESG-indebted "Baby" ("Baby, You know what's good / Baby, Make me feel good/Baby, I'm loving this mood / Baby, Nobody could"). It's possibly not surprising to hear Sil admit then that the group have previously doffed the cap to the Scroggins sisters' discography in their own live shows: "We'd been playing ESG songs for a couple of years; 'Dance,' 'My Love For You,' and 'Erase You,'"[6] she lists, enthusiastically.

The latter even appeared on their 2011 release, *Kellies*, which possessed more of a zombie surf-punk bent, seamlessly enveloping ESG's needly guitar lick in among the pogo bass lines and Gang of Four guitar skronks. Six months after the album's release, though, Las Kellies' label propositioned them with a remarkable opportunity. Fire Records released a double split for 2012s Record Store Day featuring the group's version of the track, alongside the reissued original from ESG themselves: "It was one of the most important moments for us," confesses Sil. "I don't know if there are many musicians that can have that chance in their careers." While the band no longer performs ESG covers in their set (they have six full-length releases to their name now), the Bronx-born band's sound still remains invaluable to them today.

"We are now starting to prepare the next album and we want to do something else. Something different than before with new instruments but I'm still thinking about them and the approach they have to music,"[7] continues Sil. Ceci is in agreement: "There's nothing else like the beat, the groove and even if we want to make another album, more electronic and not so rocky, we're gonna grab things from them." Over the last forty years of ESG's career and the tranches of groups and movements that their style has seeped into, their mission remains at the heart of that sound, a shared value Sil sees in Las Kellies' own work. "The most important thing is that we want to make people dance and have fun. Not in a superficial kind of way but it's really nice when we are playing live and you can see from the stage people with a smile and moving their body."[8]

In an interview together for She Shreds magazine in 2017, Renee Scroggins reflected on a similar sentiment in her hopes for the music she and her sisters were creating: "I don't like to put us in a genre or a box. We are ourselves. Whether it's just plain bass and drums or voice, we're just doing sounds that make you wanna dance."[9] These nonconformist ideals are one of the reasons why Ceci Kelly believes the band's prevalence is so far-reaching even today. "It doesn't depend on the genre, it's about the groove, the feeling, and the intention. When we play those records at a party, everybody's dancing even if they don't know them."[10]

Come Away with ESG is instinctual, possessing a primitive call to your brain's synapses to start moving, a songwriting skill Sil Kelly reasons make the sister troupe even more special. "It's not that easy to find musicians that have that kind of groove. Maybe you think it's possible, but it's not so easy to do it like *that*."[11] Yet despite their cult following and enthusiastic entourage across the globe from Manhattan to Manchester, utter the Scroggins sisters' names to a group of music fans and you'll find a fair few blank faces. So while their records might appear in the cool crates at a party and the rhythms reach across the dancefloor like creeping ivy, the track gets mixed into a postpunk counterpart, and ESG's name is lost in the crowds.

With such a multigenerational impact and a string of cult champions, why has a band like ESG remained a footnote in history then? The group's early experiences with the music industry can't have helped. Ed Bahlman's influential imprint, 99 Records, provided a platform for the band, but he knew little about recording, pressing, and distributing music. His intentions were admirable, but even winning the lawsuit with Sugar Hill Records for royalties owed, didn't prove profitable for the label's future. A bad distribution deal with MCA Records left Sugar Hill bankrupt and unable to pay. Bahlman was too broke from the legal fees to keep 99 Records open, and ESG was left without a label, management, or much of a career.

Bahlman's refusal to return the rights of the original recordings to his artists meant that while *Come Away with ESG* might have marked the band's most successful and commercial release to date, the band made minimal profits from its sales. Instead, that income stream lay solely with 99 Records and remains so to this day. This poor business structure tainted the band's experience of the record industry from a very young age. The exploitation only continued into the 1990s as the band was repeatedly victimized by uncleared samples of their material, as Renee Scroggins explained opening up to New York–based journalist, cultural critic, and friend, Carol Cooper: "Every year I get calls from various independent labels wanting to remix it, or buy it, or license it. And they always think the band is so desperate that we'll be stupid enough to release the rights to our work for little or nothing."[12]

Through hard graft and grit over decades, ESG has garnered the respect of influential figureheads (from iconic postpunk producer Martin Hannett to dance-punk revivalist James Murphy) and performed on some of the most coveted stages across the globe. But even with a tireless track record and four decades of touring and album releases under their belt, it seems that the sentiment Renee Scroggins sang about in early EP track "Earn It" never quite rang true for the group: "There ain't nothing in this life that's free / If you want some of that green money / You have to do something called work, you see / If you want some of that green money / You have to earn it." While the group's material might have been sampled into triple figures, these (often chart-topping) releases never resulted in ESG getting residuals or any recognition. The compensation structure just wasn't there for it.

While the Scroggins sisters might've felt ostracized and exploited by some of their projects peers sampling their tracks, their roaming range of influences and eclectic songwriting style gave them a free pass into the New York no-wave scene alongside fellow 99 Records signees Bush Tetras and Glenn Branca. But as was the transient nature of such a movement, by the early 1980s, a lot of the flagship bands that were heralded in the no-wave scene for their rejection of rock and roll clichés had ended up rising the ranks into the mainstream. Take Sonic Youth, their alternate tunings and throbbing basslines seeped into the sound of emerging grunge bands like Mudhoney, L7, and Nirvana. (It's worth stating that while Thurston Moore and co. broadened their listenership tenfold by signing to major label Geffen in 1990, the band did maintain its allegiances to the underground determined to introduce a whole new generation to outside music through their prominent press coverage in Spin and Rolling Stone.)

As no-wave acts began to shapeshift out of the scene and into a new wave of alt-rock and nationwide media spreads, the downtown newspapers covering the live music that surrounded ESG began closing down. As Scroggins continues to explain to Cooper, "By the late 1980s/early 1990s, European critics were more interested in covering major label acts or hyping homegrown talent."[13] With the dissolution of their 99 Records platform and the no-wave moment all but dried out, the momentum of ESG's music also waned. While other groups like Sonic Youth sidestepped out of the underground and into the limelight, the Scroggins sisters were still scrambling around in the dark.

In fact, after touring *Come Away with ESG* into the late 1980s, and left adrift without legal or managerial representation, the band took a four-year hiatus to learn enough about pressing, distributing, and publishing their own compositions before returning with their frustrations front and center in the 1992s release *Sample Credits Don't Pay Our Bills*—but to little fanfare. Whether it was the small-label distribution (*Sample Credits* ... came out via Nega Fulo Records stateside and British house/nu-jazz label Nuphonic in the UK) or the inability for critics to pigeonhole ESG's cross-pollinated party of Latin, funk, and afrobeat influences, the most that's been published about the group to date is often the story of their intersibling conflicts (Deborah sued the band in Brooklyn federal court in 2009, claiming she was not being fairly compensated for her share of the band's royalties) and Renee's ongoing battle with sampling rights and attribution.

Yeah Yeah Yeahs frontwoman Karen O weighs up the band's wide-ranging reference points as both the band's definitive calling card and also their eventual undoing: "I wonder if some of the reason ESG doesn't share the posterity of other bands from the era has to do with them being so brilliantly crossover and solely unique. Other bands that don't fit neatly into a category get sidelined, what are they? A bit post-punk, a bit hip hop, a bit disco, a bit funk." But as Orzolek rightly adds, "Who cares, they absolutely slay."[14] Or is the lack of media on the matriarchal family band a comment on a wider systemic issue with the music industry as a whole?

Until recent years, African American artists have been pigeonholed into a certain type of sound. It was difficult for Black musicians to make records that cut across genres. ESG defied all that. The Scroggins sisters' refusal to sell out and compromise their sound has given them a catalogue of genre-bending and decade-defying songs (and, as demonstrated, often inexplicably mirroring the zeitgeist at the time, like that of the noughties dance-punk revival). Again, this comes down to the authenticity of a group of sisters fresh from the Bronx creating something truly original and a future for themselves. As Renee reasons, "One of the main things is that we kept true to ourselves: we kept it minimalist, we kept it funky. I didn't try to go with what was the trend of the moment. We kept to ourselves musically."[15] By doing so, ESG hit upon a style of live dance music that remains incomparable.

Alongside the issue of genre, could it also be a question of gender? As four African American sisters at the time, ESG provided some much needed diversity in an overly masculine, and white, music scene. Orzolek considers the same: "Maybe they were taken less seriously because they were a girl group who flouted the rules of the male dominated genres they had a foot in." But regardless of their outsider positioning, those who know the band succumb to their sound readily. As Orzolek continues, "They will always stand out to me as one of the greatest NYC bands. I hear 'Erase You' on countless playlists and dance floors, their appeal is undeniable."[16]

While Orzolek might happily rate the Bronx band's musical magnetism, four decades on from their inception and the evolution of what it means to be a "success" as an artist has shifted significantly. Long gone are the local talent shows featuring community figureheads manning the judging panels with the promise of a record deal. Today, we live in a world where bedroom pop artists can rise to meteoric fame through social media snippets and bite-size storytelling. Your musical peers and homegrown heroes no longer share the same postcodes. Celebrities are entourages far away. Despite her best efforts to reassure us in the 2002 single, "Jenny from the Block," you don't see J-Lo down in St. Mary's Park even though she once called the borough home.

The Scroggins grew up in the projects, where the music was all around you. It was community based. But after those relations turned sour and their Bronx-based peers started stealing from their neighbors, both literally and metaphorically, is it any surprise that the Scroggins sisters no longer wanted to put themselves out there? Even without the artistic accolades to their name, though, they deserve quiet recognition. Author Kathy Iandoli agrees

> Maybe Renee doesn't want to be a part of the matrix. But in those circles, she needs to be held up as royalty. The flowers should be given even if she puts them in a vase in her home and just stares at them and doesn't post them on Instagram. You can't be like, 'Well, maybe she should have made herself well known.[17]

And, on that point of fame, let's close with a game-changing thought and a concept that has turned die-hard fans against their beloved indie acts for decades: Would ESG even *be* the same band if they had gone mainstream? If things had been different and they'd been given their dues and rightly credited? Their Argentinian postpunk protégées believe the band's anonymity could be less about the sisters' self-made marketing and more about the underbelly of a toxic industry: "The scene is tough and the people that are in the mainstream are put there for me. It's not because the audience wants them, it's because someone decides who the masses must hear,"[18] explains drummer Sil Kelly.

If the sisters had been picked up by a major in the 1990s, what impact would that have had on their songwriting? ESG suddenly becomes a project with multiple stakeholders, no longer driven by the family four, and some of that original integrity is lost as Ceci Kelly knows only too well: "When you are signed to a label, you have to be shaped by the label. We love our label Fire but they rejected an album that we made before *Friends and Lovers* so we understand that sometimes when you think that you have the best thing you ever made, for everyone else, it's not the same."[19] For ESG, though, *Come Away with ESG* remains one of their greatest bodies of work (second only to those early EPs).

Perhaps, then, one of the core elements that makes *Come Away with ESG* so exciting is the journey to discover the band and their story. To paraphrase Sil Kelly, an ardent DIY fan, "The real shit is always underground." As a music fan, there's a certain sense of elation stumbling upon something special like the Scroggins, a band that you're going to devote time to, replaying their records, sporting their merchandise, and finally standing in a crowd full of others rejoicing in their brilliance. ESG has been racking up that faithful following for over forty years and now you too, reader, are in one of the music industry's best kept secrets. The story of how a group of young sisters journeyed out of the South Bronx and onto the international stage to change the face of modern dance music as we know it. *Come Away with ESG* is your ticket to a seat at the Scroggins table; a fearless feast of primitive beats, headstrong lyricism, and disco diva hedonism for a new age.

Reflecting on a life-spanning legacy in 2018 for She Shreds, Renee Scroggins explained how she felt forever indebted to the band for realizing a long-standing ambition of the honorary fifth member of ESG, Helen Scroggins, and how even through all of the changes in the years that have passed, she would've been unimaginably pleased with the group's journey so far: "One of the greatest things I can say, and it truly made my Mum proud, was that we were able to travel the world with our music." Because while ESG's career has spanned over forty years, the New York club circuit that the band began performing in during the late 1970s has transformed dramatically.

With everything from counterculture institution the Mudd Club to Union Square's historic Irving Plaza, the opportunities to develop a local audience and reputation as an artist in seventies New York felt ample. But by the 1980s, only Danceteria and the Roxy were still offering live dance funk, and today, many have closed down their doors for good. Unlike the live circuit that surrounded them as teens, the Scroggins sisters are still standing, as Renee reflects, with a hearty laugh: "Some venues have come and some venues have gone. We've actually been around longer than some of the venues."[20]

In *Come Away with ESG*, ESG has immortalized that early archetype of dance funk finesse. Over the years, buildings might have fallen and music scenes might have faltered, but this groundbreaking feat of songwriting will continue to sound out for years to come—omnipresent, unstoppable, and finally making sense to those who hear it.

Notes

Introduction

1   Carol Cooper, "Emerald Sapphire & Gold: Alive, Well and Working in the South Bronx," *Dance Music Report*, September 26, 1990.

2   Kathy Iandoli, Interview with the author, July 2, 2021.

Chapter 1

1   Luis Ferré-Sadurní, "The Rise and Fall of New York Public Housing: An Oral History," *The New York Times*, July 9, 2018.

2   Peter Kihiss, "Housing Policy of City Changed," *The New York Times*, January 27, 1964.

3   Bobby Sanabria, interview with the author, March 2, 2021.

4   Joe Flood, "Why the Bronx Burned," *New York Post*, May 16, 2010.

5   Robert A. Lynn, "C'est le Bronx," *Word Reference*, August 10, 2011, https://forum.wordreference.com/threads/cest-le-bron x-cest-le-broux-sic.2219605/

6   Elena Martinez, interview with the author, March 2, 2021.

7   Bobby Sanabria, interview with the author, March 2, 2021.

8 Martin Tolchin, "Gangs Spread Terror in the South Bronx," *The New York Times*, January 16, 1973.

9 Bobby Sanabria, interview with the author, March 2, 2021.

10 Vivien Goldman, interview with the author, April 24, 2021.

11 Damien Cave, "A Young Jesse Jackson Rallies for Jobs," *The New York Times*, February 4, 2016.

12 Martin Tolchin, "Gangs Spread Terror in the South Bronx," *The New York Times*, January 16, 1973.

13 Greg Kot, "ESG Turned "Accident" into Music History," *Chicago Tribune*, May 24, 2018.

14 Bobby Sanabria, interview with the author, March 2, 2021.

15 Scenery Samundra, "A South Bronx Tale: An Interview with ESG's Renee Scroggins," *Culture Collide*, March 23, 2018.

16 Luis Ferre-Sadurni, "The Rise and Fall of New York Public Housing: An Oral History," *The New York Times*, July 9, 2018.

17 Renee Scroggins, interview with the author, October 28, 2017.

18 Renee Scroggins, interview with the author, October 28, 2017.

19 Renee Scroggins, interview with the author, October 28, 2017.

20 Greg Kot, "ESG Turned 'Accident' into Music History," *Chicago Tribune*, May 24, 2018.

21 Renee Scroggins, interview with the author, October 28, 2017.

22 Renee Scroggins, interview with the author, October 28, 2017.

23 Renee Scroggins, interview with the author, October 28, 2017.

24 Renee Scroggins, interview with the author, May 4, 2015.

25 Martin Moscrop, "Factory Records Day: Factory by a Certain Ratio's Martin Moscrop," *Drowned in Sound*, January 26, 2009.

26 Renee Scroggins, interview with the author, October 28, 2017.

27 Optimo, "Nine Nine Records," September 18, 2009.

28 Renee Scroggins, interview with the author, October 28, 2017.

29 Greg Kot, "ESG Turned 'Accident' into Music History," *Chicago Tribune*, May 24, 2018.

30 The Clash at Bond International Casino, New York City, May and June, 1981.

31 https://www.openculture.com/2021/04/how-the-clash-embraced-new-yorks-hip-hop-scene.html

   Keri Phillips, "Ed Bahlman, 99 Records Interview," *ABC Radio Australia*.

32 Renee Scroggins, interview with the author, May 4, 2015.

33 Melissa Steiner, "It's Music That Makes You Dance: ESG Interviewed," *The Quietus*, September 7, 2015.

34 Tim O'Neil, "A South Bronx Story 2," *Pop Matters*, January 27, 2008.

35 Tim O'Neil, "A South Bronx Story 2," *Pop Matters*, January 27, 2008.

36 Vivien Goldman, interview with the author, April 24, 2021.

37 Renee Scroggins, interview with the author, October 28, 2017.

Chapter 2

1 Vivien Goldman, interview with the author, April 24, 2021.

2 Tim Ross, "Something Like a Phenomenon: The Complete 99 Records Story," *The Vinyl Factory*, March 13, 2015.

3 Morgan Enos, "6 Classic Albums That Wouldn't Exist without Glennn Branca," *Billboard*, May 14, 2018.

4 Audrey J. Golden, "Bush Tetras at 40: An Interview with Drummer Dee Pop," *Louder Than War*, April 20, 2020.

5 Robert Christgau, "Party in Hard Times," *The Village Voice*, February 18, 2003.

6 Vivien Goldman, interview with the author, April 24, 2021.

7 Vivien Goldman, interview with the author, April 24, 2021.

8 Vivien Goldman, interview with the author, April 24, 2021.

9 Vivien Goldman, interview with the author, April 24, 2021.

10 Renee Scroggins, interview with the author, May 4, 2015

11 Melissa Steiner, "It's Music That Makes You Dance—ESG interviewed," *The Quietus*, September 7, 2015.

12 Ben Kelly, "Behind the Scenes of the Hacienda Opening Party," *The Vinyl Factory*, May 21, 2017.

13 Peter Hook, interview with the author, July 25, 2021.

14 Peter Hook, interview with the author, July, 25 2021.

15 Peter Hook, interview with the author, July 25, 2021.

16 Ben Kelly, "Behind the Scenes of the Hacienda Opening Party," *The Vinyl Factory*, May 21 2017.

17 Peter Hook, interview with the author, July 25, 2021.

18 Renee Scroggins, interview with the author, October 28, 2018.

19 Exhibition Companion, "Use Hearing Protection: The Early Years of Factory Records, *Science Industry Museum*, June 19, 2021–January 3, 2022.

20 Peter Hook, interview with the author, July 25, 2021.

21 Vivien Goldman, interview with the author, April 24, 2021.

22 Vivien Goldman, interview with the author, April 24, 2021.

23 Tim Ross, "Something Like a Phenomenon: The Complete 99 Records Story," *The Vinyl Factory*, March 13, 2015.

24 Vivien Goldman, interview with the author, April 24, 2021.

25 Renee Scroggins, interview with the author, October 28, 2017.

26 Vivien Goldman, interview with the author, April 24, 2021.

27 Tim Ross, "Something Like a Phenomenon: The Complete 99 Records Story," *The Vinyl Factory*, March 13, 2015.

Chapter 3

1 Greg Kot, "ESG Turned 'Accident' into Music History," *Chicago Tribune*, May 24, 2018.

2 Vivien Goldman, interview with the author, April 24, 2021.

3 Elena Martinez, interview with the author, March 2, 2021.

4 Bobby Sanabria, interview with the author, March 2, 2021.

5 Kathy Iandoli, interview with the author, July 2, 2021.

6 Kathy Iandoli, interview with the author, July 2, 2021.

7 Elena Martinez, interview with the author, March 2, 2021.

8 Bobby Sanabria, interview with the author, March 2, 2021.

9 Marc Myers, "How Chic's 'Good Times' Launched Rap," *The Wall Street Journal*, January 29, 2017.

10 Steve Hockman, "Judge Raps Practice of Sampling," *Los Angeles Times*, December 18, 1991.

11 Greg Kot, "ESG Turned 'Accident' into Music History," *Chicago Tribune*, May 24, 2018 and Bobby Sanabria, interview with the author, March 2, 2021.

12 Kathy Iandoli, interview with the author, July 2, 2021.

13 Kathy Iandoli, interview with the author, July 2, 2021.

14 Kathy Iandoli, interview with the author, July 2, 2021.

15 Kathy Iandoli, interview with the author, July 2, 2021.

16 Kathy Iandoli, interview with the author, July 2, 2021.

17 Jimmy Ness, "A Conversation with Enya about Sampling, the Nature of Fame, and How to Control Your Fear," *Forbes*, June 20, 2016.

18 Garry Mulholland, "ESG; Ma Scroggins' girls," *The Independent*, August 23, 2002.

19 "Enya Takes on the Fugees," *Irish Voice*, February 18, 1997, https://web.archive.org/web/20050407183319/http://www.enya.org/p_trans4/b019.htm (a web archive article from the *Philadelphia Inquirer* that has been transcribed by Edelmiro Garcia).

20 Renee Scroggins, interview with the author, May 4, 2015.

21 Renee Scroggins, interview with the author, May 4, 2015.

22 Renee Scroggins, interview with the author, May 4, 2015.

23 Jessica Meiselman, "Sampled or Stolen? Untangling the Knotty World of Hip Hop Copyright," *FACT*, June 25, 2016.

24 Kathy Iandoli, interview with the author, July 2, 2021.

Chapter 4

1 Matt Saincome, "Legendary Band ESG's Career Finale at Hard French Pride Weekend Blowout," *San Francisco Examiner*, June 24, 2015.

2 Renee Scroggins, interview with the author, May 4, 2015.

3 Scenery Samundra, "A South Bronx Tale: An Interview with ESG's Renee Scroggins," *Culture Collide*, March 23, 2018.

4 Adrienne Day, "The Records That Changed My Life," *SPIN*, February 2005.

5 John Doran, "Soundsystem and Vision," *ireallylovemusic.com*, archived January 17, 2006.

6 Karen O(rzolek), interview with the author, June 22, 2021.

7 Karen O(rzolek), interview with the author, June 22, 2021.

8 Karen O(rzolek), interview with the author, June 22, 2021.

9 Karen O(rzolek), interview with the author, June 22, 2021.

10 Renee Scroggins, interview with the author, May 8, 2015.

11 Anne Gallien, interview with the author, October 21, 2021.

12 Anne Gallien, interview with the author, October 21, 2021.

13 Anne Gallien, interview with the author, October 21, 2021.

14 Anne Gallien, interview with the author, October 21, 2021.

15 Anne Gallien, interview with the author, October 21, 2021.

16 Anne Gallien, interview with the author, October 21, 2021.

17 Anne Gallien, interview with the author, October 21, 2021.

18 Anne Gallien, interview with the author, October 21, 2021.

Chapter 5

1 Elena Martinez, interview with the author, March 2, 2021.

2 Michael Diamond and Adam Horovitz, "Danceteria Playlist," *Beastie Boys Book*, 2018.

3 Kathy Iandoli, interview with the author, July 2, 2021.

4 Chris Dalen, "Liars: They Threw Us All in a Trench and Stuck a Monument on Top," *Pitchfork*, July 17, 2002.

5 Ceci Kelly, interview with the author, January 21, 2022.

6 Sil Kelly, interview with the author, January 21, 2022.

7 Sil Kelly, interview with the author, January 21, 2022.

8 Ceci Kelly, interview with the author, January 21, 2022.

9 Renee Scroggins, interview with the author, October 28, 2017.

10 Ceci Kelly, interview with the author, January 21, 2022.

11 Sil Kelly, interview with the author, January 21, 2022.

12 Carol Cooper, "Emerald Sapphire & Gold: Alive, Well and Working in the South Bronx," *Dance Music Report*, September 26, 1990.

13 Carol Cooper, "Emerald Sapphire & Gold: Alive, Well and Working in the South Bronx," *Dance Music Report*, September 26, 1990.

14 Karen O, interview with the author, June 22, 2021.

15 Renee Scroggins, interview with the author, October 28, 2018.

16 Karen O, interview with the author, June 22, 2021.

17 Kathy Iandoli, interview with the author, July 2, 2021.

18 Sil Kelly, interview with the author, January 21, 2022.

19 Ceci Kelly, interview with the author, January 21, 2022.

20 Renee Scroggins, interview with the author, October 28, 2018.

Also Available